Value of Information: Intellectual Property, Privacy and Big Data

Lex et Res Publica
Polish Legal and Political Studies
Edited by Anna Jaroń

Volume 7

Zur Qualitätssicherung und Peer Review der vorliegenden Publikation

Die Qualität der in dieser Reihe erscheinenden Arbeiten wird vor der Publikation durch den Herausgeber der Reihe geprüft.

Notes on the quality assurance and peer review of this publication

Prior to publication, the quality of the work published in this series is reviewed by the editors of the series.

Maciej Barczewski

Value of Information: Intellectual Property, Privacy and Big Data

Bibliographic Information published by the Deutsche Nationalbibliothek
The Deutsche Nationalbibliothek lists this publication
in the Deutsche Nationalbibliografie; detailed bibliographic
data is available in the internet at http://dnb.d-nb.de.
Library of Congress Cataloging-in-Publication Data
Names: Barczewski, Maciej, editor.
Title: Value of information : intellectual property, privacy and big data /
Maciej Barczewski (editor).
Description: Berlin ; New York : Peter Lang, 2018. | Series: Lex et res
publica : Polish legal and political studies ; V 7
Identifiers: LCCN 2018024084 | ISBN 9783631750131
Subjects: LCSH: Intellectual property. | Data protection--Law and legislation
| Privacy, Right of. | Big data. | European Parliament. Regulation (EU)
2016/679 of the European Parliament and of the Council of 27 April 2016 on
the protection of natural persons with regard to the processing of personal
data and on the free movement of such data, and repealing Directive
95/46/EC (General Data Protection Regulation) | Intellectual property--
European Union countries. | Data protection--Law and legislation--
European Union countries. | Privacy, Right of--European Union countries.
Classification: LCC K1401 .V35 2018 | DDC 346.2404/8--dc23
LC record available at https://lccn.loc.gov/2018024084

Publication co-financed by the Faculty of Law and
Administration of the University of Gdansk.

Cover Design: © Olaf Gloeckler, Atelier Platen, Friedberg

ISSN 2191-3250
ISBN 978-3-631-75013-1 (Print)
E-ISBN 978-3-653-76063-5 (E-Book)
E-ISBN 978-3-631-76064-2 (EPUB)
E-ISBN 978-3-63176065-9 (MOBI)
DOI 10.3726/14335

© Peter Lang GmbH
International Academic Publishers
Berlin 2018
All rights reserved.

Peter Lang – Berlin · Bern · Bruxelles · New York ·
Oxford · Warszawa · Wien

All parts of this publication are protected by copyright. Any utilisation outside
the strict limits of the copyright law, without the permission of the publisher, is
forbidden and liable to prosecution. This applies in particular to reproductions,
translations, microfilming, and storage and processing in electronic retrieval systems.

This publication has been peer reviewed

www.peterlang.com

Contents

List of Contributors 7

Andreas Wiebe
Protection of Non-Personal Data: A New Legal Framework for
Data Ownership? 9

Edward Carter
Big Data, Criminal Jurisdiction, and Transnational Crime: How
the Long Arm of the Law Reaches across National Borders 27

Arkadiusz Lach
Identity Theft in the European Union: Do We Need Harmonization? 43

Joanna Marszałek
Identity Theft in the United States: A Different Perspective? 59

Maciej Barczewski and Aleksandra Czubek
Wearable Technology: Selected Legal Challenges Related to Big
Data Collection 73

Dagmara Jaroszewska-Choraś and Sebastian Sykuna
Selected Legal Regulations Concerning Biometrics and
the Biometric Data 101

Maciej Zejda
Applicable Law and Jurisdiction in Data Protection Law: Values
behind the Source of Data Protection 121

Richard Warner and Robert H. Sloan
Defending Our Data: The Need for Information We Do Not Have 149

List of Contributors

Maciej Barczewski
Dr hab., professor at the University of Gdańsk, Head of Centre for Intellectual Property Law

Edward Carter
Assistant, Illinois Attorney General

Aleksandra Czubek
Assistant professor at the University of Gdańsk, Centre for Intellectual Property Law

Dagmara Jaroszewska-Choraś
Assistant Professor of Law, Faculty of Administration and Social Sciences, Kazimierz Wielki University, Bydgoszcz

Arkadiusz Lach
Prof. dr hab. Arkadiusz Lach, Department of Criminal Procedure, Cybercrime Research Centre, Faculty of Law and Administration, Nicolaus Copernicus University in Torun, Poland

Joanna Marszałek
Assistant Professor, Centre for Intellectual Property Law, Faculty of Law and Administration, University of Gdańsk

Robert H. Sloan
Professor and Head, Department of Computer Science, University of Illinois at Chicago. Partially supported by National Science Foundation Grant No. DGE-1069311

Sebastian Sykuna
Dr hab., professor at the University of Gdańsk, Head of the Department of Human Rights and Legal Ethics

Richard Warner
Professor of Law, Chicago-Kent College of Law, Visiting Foreign Professor, University of Gdańsk, Poland

Prof. Dr. Andreas Wiebe
LL.M. (Virginia), Chair for Civil Law, Intellectual Property Law, Media Law and Information and Communications Technology Law at the Georg-August-University of Göttingen

Maciej Zejda
Research and teaching assistant, Faculty of Law and Administration, University of Gdańsk

Andreas Wiebe

Protection of Non-Personal Data: A New Legal Framework for Data Ownership?[1]

1 Introduction

The establishment of data economy is high on the political agenda, and part of the Digital Single Market Strategy for Europe is the establishment of harmonized legal rules on data ownership.[2] While the protection of personal data goes back to the sixties and seventies, the issue of protection of nonpersonal or industrial data has emerged only recently. With an enormous increase of digitization in all areas of the society and economy, the production, collection, and reusing of data is exploding in all fields. Big Data, the Internet of Things and services, robots, and an intensified vertical integration of companies with increased data networks as the backbone of production and services ("smart factory")[3] are the main trends. Within this environment, a huge bulk of data will be produced, aggregated, and distributed, including sensor and machine-generated data and machine-to-machine exchange of data. New business models will emerge (esp. for SME), and new and highly specialized services are expected.

The lack of a proper legal framework is often referred to as a potential impediment and the need for a free flow of data is stressed.[4] In 2015, Commissioner Oettinger announced that the first step in the data strategy of the European Union (EU) would be to create a legal basis clarifying who owns data: "We need a virtual and digital law of property that includes data."[5]

---

1 This chapter is based on A. Wiebe, *Protection of industrial data – a new property right for the digital economy?*, Journal of Intellectual Property Law & Practice, 2017, vol. 12(1), pp. 62–71.
2 EC, *Regions: A Digital Single Market Strategy for Europe*, COM (2015), 192 final.
3 C. Chirco, *Industrie 4.0 in der Praxis*, [in:] J. Taeger, (Hrsg.), *Internet der Dinge – Digitalisierung von Wirtschaft und Gesellschaft*, Tagungsband Herbstakademie 2015, pp. 519–520.
4 See the free flow of data initiative of the EU, COM (2015) 192 final, p. 17.
5 Commissioner Oettinger, Speech at Hannover Fair, April 2015, p. 41 http://www.compliancedigital.de/.download/123622/zfc_20150202.pdf (visited April 20, 2018).

While a large quantity of these data could still be considered to be person-related and thus regulated by the rules of data protection law, data are increasingly sensored or produced by humans or machines and do not qualify as personal data. Nevertheless, these data are essential for the economy in many ways and are being exchanged or traded as digital goods. Here, consumers and entrepreneurs are producers of data while their analysis is a business feature. If one looks at contracts or standard terms, what can be very often found is that "property rights" in such data are transferred and consequently these data are treated as if an intellectual property protection existed. In reality, however, there are no regulations exclusively pertaining to data as such. Therefore, it is barely surprising that at some point the issue came up of whether there is a need for creating an intellectual property right for nonpersonal data, or whether the existing legal framework is sufficient. The EU Commission now put this topic on the agenda and issued a Communication with an accompanying, thoroughly elaborated, staff document, which outlines some alternatives in approaching the topic.[6] After a stakeholder process in the first half of 2017, an outcome is expected for 2018.

In the academic field, there has been some discussion in recent years about developing data protection rules into some kind of a property right. The issue here, however, is much broader and focuses on industrial data and a different balance of interests needed in this field.[7] Hence, this issue will be discussed

---

6   EC, *Communication Building a European Data Economy*, COM (2017) 9 final of 10th January 2017; Commission Staff Working Document on the free flow of data and emerging issues of the European data economy, SWD (2017) 2 final of 10th January 2017.

7   This discussion still seems to be largely a German discussion, see H. Zech, *Information als Schutzgegenstand*, Tuebingen 2012; T. Hoeren, *Dateneigentum - Versuch einer Anwendung von § 303a StGB im Zivilrecht*, Multimedia und Recht, 2013, p. 486; M. Dorner, *"Big Data" und Dateneigentum*, Computer und Recht, 2014, p. 617; J. Sahl, *Daten als Basis der digitalen Wirtschaft und Gesellschaft*, Recht der Datenverarbeitung, 2015, p. 236; R. Schwartmann, C. Hentsch, *Eigentum an Daten – Das Urheberrecht als Pate für ein Datenverwertungsrecht*, Recht der Datenverarbeitung, 2015, p. 221; H. Zech, *Daten als Wirtschaftsgut – Überlegungen zu einem "Recht des Datenerzeugers*, Computer und Recht, 2015, p. 137; E. Hornung, C. Goeble, *"Data Ownership" im vernetzten Automobil*, Computer und Recht, 2015, p. 265. P. Bräutigam, T. Klindt, *Digitalisierte Wirtschaft/Industrie 4.0*, Expert Opinion, 2015, http://bdi.eu/media/themenfelder/digitalisierung/downloads/20151117_Digitalisierte_Wirtschaft_Industrie_40_Gutachten_der_Noerr_LLP.pdf (visited April 20, 2018); L. Specht, *Ausschließlichkeitsrechte an Daten, Notwendigkeit, Schutzumfang, Alternativen*, Computer und Recht, 2016, p. 288.

separately from the framework of data protection that culminated in the recent passing of the Data Protection Regulation.[8]

An instructive example that is already very real today is the networked car, which will eventually merge into an automated car. Already a car is equipped with a lot of sensors and an average of 80 steering devices.[9] These collect data on the state of the car, the behavior of the driver, heartbeat, alcohol, traffic, and external conditions. Different parties could be interested in these data:

- Owner of the car
- User of the car (data input)
- Navigation and Telecommunications Services
- Insurances ("pay as you drive")
- Internet Service Providers (distribution channel, data collection for advertising, growth potential € 80 bln. 2015-20)
- Government (traffic control, eCall, toll system, crime prevention)

Various conflicts between different stakeholders could be envisaged that include the issues of whether the owner of the car is entitled to prohibit the producer from collecting data in the car, or alternatively of whether he or she may allow a third party access against the will of the producer. The question is whether we can solve these conflicts under the existing regulations or whether we need a new kind of property right covering industrial data as such.

2 Protection of industrial data under existing law

2.1 Current Intellectual Property Schemes

First, we will have to examine existing intellectual property schemes in terms of the extent to which they could be applicable to data as such.

2.1.1 Copyright

Copyright is in most jurisdictions limited to information created by humans and a protected work has to be characterized by a minimum of creativity or

---

8   European Parliament and Council 2016/679 on the protection of natural persons with regard to the processing of personal data and on the free movement of such data, and repealing Directive 95/46/EC (General Data Protection Regulation), 2016/679 of 27 April 2016, OJ L 119/1.
9   See the following: G. Hornung, T. Goeble, *"Data Ownership" im vernetzten Automobil*, Computer und Recht, 2015, p. 265 et seqq.

individuality. As such, it would cover a rather limited part of the relevant data considered here. "Raw data" measured by sensors or produced by machines would not be covered, save for rare cases where automatic production already involves sufficient creativity given to the software designer.

2.1.2 Sui generis database protection

More relevant is the Directive on the protection of databases with its two-tier protection scheme.[10] In the scientific and technical field, copyright protection relating to the individual structure of a database is not so relevant. However, the sui generis protection scheme protecting the investment in setting up and maintaining databases is more important. While the threshold of relevant investment is not so hard to meet, the scheme has other shortcomings, which limit its appropriateness to cover a perceived need for the protection of nonpersonal data.

First, it does not protect data as such but only data originating from a protected database. This excludes data that are measured by sensors or machine-produced in the first phase of their existence. However, a database will most likely be present very soon after the production of the data. In this case, no protection will apply during the time span between the generation of data and their collection. Enhancing this gap is a strong case law of the Court of Justice of the European Union (CJEU), which stressed the importance of a strict separation between the generation and collection of data and excluded any investment into the generation of data from being accounted for in the course of determining sufficient investment into a database as a requirement for protection.[11] This exclusion of "spin-offs" is quite relevant in the industry 4.0 environment, where data are often produced as a by-product.[12]

This delineation is rather blurry and unconvincing. In the German doctrine, a line is drawn between data that already exist and could theoretically be measured

---

10 European Parliament and the Council Directive 96/9/EC on legal protection of databases of 11 March 1996, OJ L 77.
11 CJEU, C-203/02 n. 31 – BHB v. William Hill; C-338/02, Fixtures Marketing Ltd v. Svenska Spel AB, n. 19–38; C-444/02, Fixtures Marketing Ltd v. Organismos prognostikon agonon podosfairou AE (OPAP), n. 38–53; C-46/02, Fixtures Marketing Ltd v. Oy Veikkaus Ab, n. 34–49. See also: M. Leistner, *The Protection of Databases*, in: E. Derclaire (ed.), *Research Handbook on the Future of EU Copyright*, 2009, pp. 427, 438.
12 H. Zech, "*Industrie 4.0*" – *Rechtsrahmen für eine Datenwirtschaft im digitalen Binnenmarkt*, Gewerblicher Rechtsschutz und Urheberrecht, 2015, pp. 1151–1158.

and collected by anybody, and data that are only know to the producer.[13] As regards the first category, it is still reasonable to argue that this is the collection and not generation of data. Hence, e.g., the efforts to gather meteorological data can still be regarded as a relevant collection of data, as these data already exist in nature and may be collected by anybody. This leaves outside the scope of relevant investments for a database only data directly produced by machines.

Sui generis database protection is also closer to the use relevant in Big Data contexts by referring to data and other independent elements, as it covers aggregated, reused, and refined data and combinations of data. In the recent Esterbauer case, the CJEU considered individual elements of a street map to be relevant elements of a protected database.[14] The Court acknowledged that the informational value is always dependent on the specific context in which information is put, and the fact that it is taken out of one database and loses some value in the process is balanced by the fact that it gains value again in another context. If some loosening of the restrictive line of case law of the CJEU takes place, the database right has some potential to cover the perceived need for the protection of industrial data.[15]

Some problems remain as regards the scope of the sui generis right under Art. 7(1) of the Database Directive. It is limited to taking and reusing "substantial" parts of a database in the first place, which has been interpreted as relating to parts that required substantial investment.[16] In the second step, even taking insubstantial parts may be relevant, but the Directive requires "repeated and systematic extraction" and in addition a weighing of commercial interests, which will be even more difficult to establish. In any case, the database owner will have to demonstrate that what transpired was an extraction from his database rather than an independent creation of sources, which will be increasingly difficult in a networked environment.

A serious shortcoming of this protection scheme is that it is limited to Europe. Other parts of the world consult theories of misappropriation, which, however, are not specifically defined and far from covering an exclusive right.[17]

---

13 A. Wandtke, W. Bullinger – Thum. Hermes, UrhG, 4th ed. 2015, § 87a Rz 49; Leistner Urteilsanmerkung zu EuGH BHB v William Hill, Juristenzeitung (JZ) 2005, 408; Ct. App. Cologne, Dec. 15.12.2006, 6 U 229/05, MMR 2007, 443 – DWD-Wetterdaten.
14 CJEU, C-490/14, Judgment 29 Oct 2015 – Freistaat Bayern v. Verlag Esterbauer GmbH.
15 A. Wiebe, *Schutz von Maschinendaten durch das sui-generis-Recht für Datenbanken*, GRUR, 2017, p. 338.
16 CJEU, C-203/02 n. 70 et seq. – BHB v. William Hill.
17 U.S. *INS.v AP*, 248 U.S. 215 (1018).

The same is true for theories of unfair competition, which relate to free riding on competitors´ investments and seem to be a rather shaky ground for the protection of industrial data. In Germany, the Supreme Court has almost eliminated this theory in unfair competition law.[18] By extending this scheme, a flexible instrument could be created in case law. However, it would lack the legal certainty of a property rights scheme, and again there is a huge diversity of unfair competition law schemes worldwide, as well as lack of international conventions.

2.2 Relative protection

Some of the legal measures in place cover information in a more relative way, distinguishing these measures from absolute protection by way of a property right. "Classical" intellectual property could be characterized as providing a positive specified right in information or parts of it as such, a right to exclude third parties, and a legal mechanism to transfer the right.

2.2.1 Know-how protection

Although the protection of trade secrets and know-how has some features of property, it is based on factual secrecy. Protection depends on technical, organizational, as well as contractual measures sufficient to preserve the nonobviousness of information.[19] Under the new Directive on Protection of know-how and trade secrets passed by the European Parliament and the Council in April and May 2016, "reasonable steps under the circumstances" are required to keep the information secret.[20] It remains to be seen how much effort will be required from the owner under such a standard.

In the age of Big Data, it seems that any data collected may gain value through the possibilities of data analysis, so there may be no trivial information any more that would fall outside the scope of protection in this respect.[21] The problem

---

18 German Supreme Court, Dec. of 28 Oct. 2010, I ZR 60/09, n. 31 - Hartplatzhelden.de.
19 M. Dorner, *"Big Data" und Dateneigentum*… pp. 617–621.
20 Art. 2 (1)(c) of the Directive on the protection of undisclosed know-how and business information (trade secrets) against their unlawful acquisition, use and disclosure, 2013/0402 (COD), April 26, 2016, http://data.consilium.europa.eu/doc/document/PE-76-2015-INIT/en/pdf.
21 European Parliament and the Council Directive 2016/943 on the protection of undisclosed know – how and business information (trade secrets) against their unlawful

with trade secret protection, however, is that it does not grant an absolute right in information but is based on the preservation of factual secrecy. Once secrecy is lost, legal protection is lost as well.

Pursuing a Big Data analysis on secret information would usually require disclosure and could thus constitute infringement, even where the scope of protection is limited by the permission of independent discovery or creation as well as the permission of reverse engineering under Art. 3 of the Directive. In addition to this relative protection, from a practical point of view, it will be more difficult to keep information secret in a networked environment which is developing with the Internet of Things or industry 4.0. It will be more and more difficult to separate the spheres of different companies.

In a digital networked economy, the problem of the allocation of trade secret rights will intensify. Pursuant to Art. 2(2) of the Directive, a trade secret holder is defined as a person who "controls" a trade secret. Who would that be: the producer or provider of a machine collecting data, or its user, who may be the owner of the factory? Moreover, in the context of an unlimited flow of data between companies, the value of contracts as an effective means of protection will decrease with the number of people with access. Protection will be largely dependent on technical means of protection. As a consequence, it has to be verified in each case whether these means may be sufficient to prevent ready accessibility by the many persons and companies involved along the data processing chain. Of course, the enforcement of trade secret protection would make access to information more difficult for consumers as well as businesses from outside.

2.2.2 *Data protection*

Data protection law is applicable to information that is related to natural persons and thus covers only parts of the whole universe of data. It gives only a specific set of remedies conditioned mostly upon a weighing of interests, which has a different quality than an exclusive right to information.[22] In Germany, there is some discussion about extending data protection law into some kind of a tradable exclusive right, either by case law or legislative action.[23] However,

---

acquisition, use and Disclosure (Trade Secret Directive) of 8 June 2016 OJ L 157, Rec. 14.
22 H. Zech, *"Industrie 4.0" – Rechtsrahmen für eine Datenwirtschaft im digitalen Binnenmarkt,...*, pp. 1151–1155.
23 W. Kilian, *Strukturwandel der Privatheit*, in: H. Garstka W. Coy (eds.), *Gedächtnisschrift Steinmüller*, 2014, pp. 195–205 et seqq.; B. Buchner, *Informationelle Selbstbestimmung im Privatrecht*, 2006, p. 202 et seqq.; K-H. Ladeur, *Datenschutz – vom Abwehrrecht zur*

the strong personality aspect involved seems to undermine any efforts in this direction.[24]

2.3 Indirect protection

Further types of protection will only affect data indirectly. For some time, the protection of information in the ICT world was closely connected to the data carrier. In contracts as well as in tort, the carrier and its contents were treated as a unit and conventional legal theories relating to physical possession and property could be applied to information as well. With information increasingly detached from a carrier (e.g., cloud computing), this no longer works and is not an option for the future.

Another form of indirect protection applies in the case of technical protection measures, which may increase in importance in the future. With the legal protection of such measures laid down in the Information Society Directive,[25] information could be protected against unauthorized access by somebody dismantling the technical protection measures.

2.4 General civil law concepts

Beyond the schemes of intellectual property and related concepts, another option is to seek protection in the framework of traditional civil law concepts.[26] Protection under general tort law[27] would be limited to destruction and

---

planerischen Optimierung von Wissensnetzwerken, DuD 2000, pp. 12–18; L. Specht, *Konsequenzen der Ökonomisierung informationeller Selbstbestimmung*, 2016, p. 76. As to the economic side see P. Samuelson, *Privacy as Intellectual Property*, Stanford Law Review, 2000, p. 1125; P. Schwartz, *Property, Privacy, and Personal Data*, Harvard Law Review, 2004, p. 2056; W. Kerber, *Digital Markets, Data, and Privacy*, Competition Law, Consumer Law, and Data Protection, Gewerblicher Rechtsschutz und Urheberrecht, Internationaler Teil, 2016, p. 639 et seqq.

24 A. Roßnagel, *Big Data – Small Privacy?*, Zeitschrift für Datenschutz, 2013, p. 562; G. Hornung T. Goeble, *"Data Ownership" im vernetzten Automobil*, Computer und Recht, 2015, pp. 265–269.

25 Art. 6 and 7 of the European Parliament and of the Council Directive 2001/29/EC on the harmonisation of certain aspects of copyright and related rights in the information society of 22 May 2001 OJ L 167/10.

26 M. Dorner, *"Big Data" und Dateneigentum*, Computer und Recht, 2014, p. 617 et seq., H. Zech, *Daten als Wirtschaftsgut – Überlegungen zu einem "Recht des Datenerzeugers"*, Computer und Recht, 2015, p. 137 et seq.

27 K. Meier, A. Wehlau, *Neue Juristische Wochenschrift*, 1998, 1585, 1588; M. Bartsch, *Daten als Rechtsgut nach § 823 Abs. 1 BGB*, in: I. Conrad, M. Grützmacher (eds.), *Recht der*

modification, but would not include copying or use, which places it far from the main features of property rights.[28] In part, this protection is still dependent on the presence of a data carrier.[29]

The next step would be to establish a property right in data based on general civil law property.[30] Again, the power of factual exclusion is taken as a reference point to establish this kind of property. Basically, the analogy to civil law property, where possession is a central concept of property in rem, does not hold in a world of information, which is detached from carriers and does not show the publicity function attached to bodily things.[31]

To sum up, the current legal framework does not provide any form of protection to data as such that is comparable to an intellectual property right. Thus, the question is: do we need such a right and what could it look like?

3 Proposals for a new property right in data

Due to the perceived deficiencies of the current legal framework, there have been calls for establishing a new property right in data which could be classified as a kind of a neighboring right. What could it look like?

The most important as well as most difficult task in IP law is to strike the proper balance between the level of protection needed to create incentives and the proper leeway to guarantee access to information ("fine tuning"). There have been some proposals concerning the specific design of such a data right.[32]

Daten und Datenbanken im Unternehmen, 2014, pp. 297–300; German Supreme Court, Dec. of 2 July 1996, X ZR 64/94, Computer und Recht, 1996, p. 663 - Optikprogramm.
28 In the U.S. there has been a long standing discussion on the appropriateness of a property vs. a liability rule, see *Guido Calabresi/A. Douglas Melamed*, Property Rules, Liability Rules, and Inalienability: One View of the Cathedral, 85 Harvard Law Review, 1089 (1972); M. Krauss, *Property Rules vs. Liability Rules*, 2 Encyclopedia of Law and Economics, p. 782 (Boudewijn ouckaert & Gerrit De Geest, eds., 2000), available at http://encyclo.findlaw.com/3800book.pdf. (visited April 20, 2018).
29 Court of Appeals Karlsruhe, Dec. of 7 Nov. 1995, 3 U 15/95, Computer und Recht 1996, 352; Court of Appeals Oldenburg, Dec. of 24 Nov. 2011, 2 U 98/11, Computer und Recht 2012, p. 77.
30 T. Hoeren, Dateneigentum - Versuch einer Anwendung von § 303a StGB im Zivilrecht... p. 486 et seq. See also Court of Appels Naumburg, Dec. of 27 Aug. 2014, 6 U 3/15, Computer und Recht, 2016, p. 83.
31 As to the special characteristics of information, H. Spinner, *Wissensordnung*, 1994, p. 28 et seq.; J. Kohler, *Die Idee des geistigen Eigentums*, AcP, 1894, vol. 82, pp. 153–157.
32 H. Zech, *Information als Schutzgegenstand*, 2012, p. 421 et seq.; H. Zech, "*Industrie 4.0*" - *Rechtsrahmen für eine Datenwirtschaft im digitalen Binnenmarkt...*,

Protection should be conditioned on the "coding" of data, which refers to generation or first storage or recording.[33] The next step would be to limit the subject matter by some requirement of added value or novelty.[34] Added value would require a substantive valuation, which seems quite impossible in light of the various kinds of information in the context of Big Data. With respect to novelty, however, the analysis could draw on the question of whether these data have been created or stored before. In this respect, it is relevant that data are an abstract concept that has to be separated from its physical embodiment. We would need some help from information science to establish concepts which could enable us to meaningfully identify "new" data. The only qualifying criterion which would be easier to verify is investment, incomparable to the sui generis database protection.

The next issue to be solved in drafting a new right is that of who data rights should be allocated to. In a digital environment, there are many stakeholders, as the example with the car has shown. One basic decision would relate to the issue of whether to limit such a right to entrepreneurs or commercial entities or to include consumers as possible rightholders as well. Much will depend on whether personal data will be included in such a scheme, and hence, an adjustment to data protection law would be necessary.

Further limitations are stipulated as to the scope of a data right.[35] It should be limited to the copying of the already existing data, including statistical analysis. Consequently, generating the same data again or new data should be free. It should be limited in duration, e.g., five years, with a possibility of prolonging it. This would be drawing on the discussion concerning the duration of copyright being much too long in the digital world.[36] On the other hand, in trademark law, the possibility of prolongation provides an appropriate balance. Moreover,

---

pp. 1151–1159 et seq.; M. Becker, *Schutzrechte an Maschinendaten und die Schnittstelle zum Personendatenschutz*, in: E. Bücher et al. (eds.), *Festschrift Fezer*, 2016, pp. 815–823 et seq.

33 H. Zech, *Information als Schutzgegenstand*,... p. 427 et seq. There are parallels to the neighboring rights in photographs and sound recordings.

34 H. Zech, Information als Schutzgegenstand, 2012, p. 429 et seq.

35 *Ibidem*, p. 431.

36 R. Pollock, *Optimal Copyright over Time: Technological Change and the Stock of Works*, Cambridge University 2007, http://web.archive.org/web/20130221124708/http://rufuspollock.org/economics/papers/optimal_copyright_over_time.pdf (visited April 20, 2018).

the registration of such rights via the Internet could create some certainty in the implementation and appears to be feasible, given the state of today's technology.

Further limitation could refer to commercial exploitation, excluding the private use from its scope. While there are many problems of delineation, e.g., in determining the scope of certain Creative Commons licenses,[37] such limitation makes sense as the right should apply to industrial data. However, in the digital economy, the delineation between the commercial and the private is increasingly blurred, as can be seen in the sectors of the emerging share economy.[38] Last but not least, the use of data for scientific purposes should not be covered, which would be in accordance with the needs perceived as compelling in copyright law and acknowledged all over the different IPR schemes.

4 Evaluation

4.1 Fundamental rationale and problems

There are different rationales fundamental to intellectual property protection. While the strongest one is the incentive function, applied do data rights, evidence seems to suggest that no such right is needed, as data are created in huge volumes even without such a right. As to the disclosure function, it appears to be increasingly difficult to keep information secret in a digital economy. On the other hand, the use of technological protection would probably not be reduced by creation of such a right, as the parallel use of copyright and technology in computer software and music files has shown in the past.

So, a third rationale may be the most valid here: the allocation of a right could bring some order into a market that now looks more like the wild west. This does not mean that we would necessarily need a new right to establish markets in data, as they already do well without such a right. However, in economic terms, a legal right could have the effect of internalizing externalities and increase the efficiency of data markets.[39] Looking at personal data, as much data as possible are

---

37 T. Kreutzer, *Open-Content-Lizenzen*, Bonn 2011, https://irights.info/wp-content/uploads/userfiles/DUK_opencontent_FINAL.pdf, p. 42 et seq. (visited April 20, 2018).
38 C. Meller-Hannich, *Zu einigen rechtlichen Aspekten der "Share Economy"*, Wertpapier-Mitteilungen Zeitschrift für Wirtschafts- und Bankrecht 2014, p. 2337 et seqq.; N. Wimmer, Der Fall Uber – ein Lehrstück in Sachen Sharing Economy?, MultiMedia und Recht 2014, p. 713 et seq.
39 H. Demsetz, *Toward a Theory of Public Goods*, 57 American Economic Review 1967, pp. 347, 450; K. Arrow, in: *The Rate and Direction of Inventive Activity*, National Bureau of Economic Research, 1962, p. 609 et seq. republished in Lamberton (ed.), Economics of Information and Knowledge, 1971.

collected today by internet companies and traded without any effective restriction.[40] If there were to be a property right of the individual in his data for which the collecting companies would have to pay, they would carefully consider the quantity and quality of data worth collecting and paying for. This would create more efficiency in the interest of all stakeholders.[41] Moreover, it could enhance certainty and transparency as to the beneficiaries of data.[42] This reasoning could be transferred to industrial data as well.

On the other hand, there are three main arguments against establishing such a new property right, which are additionally intertwined:

- A paradigm shift in the protection of information
- The problem of delineating other IPR
- The problem of specification and allocation

As to the first point, IP protection is a system of *numerus clausus*, which means that there are clearly defined, limited schemes of protection, outside which the use of information is free. With a data right, this could change. The following analysis is intended to specify this point.

4.2 The distinction between data and information

It is fundamental for the whole topic to acknowledge the importance of keeping the basic distinction between data and information, which is an aspect often neglected in the legal debate as well as in legislation.[43] Data is just information in the stage of storage and transport. To illustrate this point, I would like to refer to semiotics.[44] In semiotics, the notion of information is structured according to three levels:

---

40 For an economic analysis of privacy W. Kerber, *Digital Markets, Data, and Privacy*, Competition Law, Consumer Law, and Data Protection, Gewerblicher Rechtsschutz und Urheberrecht, Internationaler Teil, 2016, p. 639.
41 W. Kilian, *Strukturwandel der Privatheit*, in: H. Garstka W. Coy (eds.), Gedächtnisschrift Steinmüller…, pp. 195, 212 et seq.; P. Samuelson, Privacy as Intellectual Property…, p. 1125 et seq.
42 H. Zech, *"Industrie 4.0" – Rechtsrahmen für eine Datenwirtschaft im digitalen Binnenmarkt*…, p. 1159.
43 D. Pombriant, *Data, Information, Knowledge*, CRi, 2013, p. 97; L. Specht, Ausschließlichkeitsrechte an Daten, Notwendigkeit, Schutzumfang, Alternativen…, p. 290.
44 R. Carnap, *Introduction to Semantics*, 3rd ed. 1948.

- Syntactics
- Semantics
- Pragmatics

Syntactics refers to the level of signs (like 0 and 1) structured according to certain rules, whereas semantics denotes the level of meaning. On the upper level, pragmatics refers to the goal that is pursued by information.

For our analysis, it is worthwhile to undertake a semiotic analysis of IPR to address the question on which level the protected elements can be allocated. The following scheme emerges:[45]

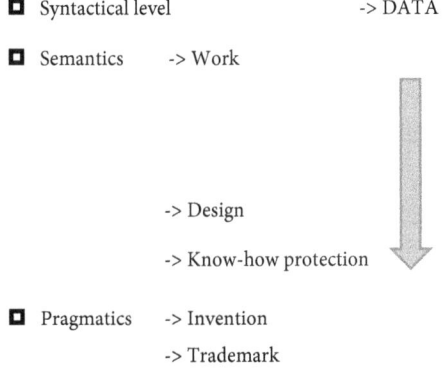

It shows that the existing schemes of IP protection can be allocated either on the level of semantics or pragmatics. IPR protection of data would be allocated to the level of syntactics. If protection were to be already attached at the level of syntactics, it would at least indirectly affect the level of semantics and pragmatics and hence have a strong chilling effect on the access to and the use of information. To give an example: copyright refers only to certain aspects of information, e.g., the creative elements in a drawing of a certain landscape. It will be protected against copying in the form of data as part of the scope of exclusive rights, but on the semantic level of subject matter, the use of the motive and noncreative elements will be free. In contrast, the protection of data as a subject matter would not take account of the contents but would foreclose access to data and at least indirectly monopolize the information on all three levels of the semiotic information concept.

---

45 A. Wiebe, *Information als Schutzgegenstand im System des geistigen Eigentums*, in: K. Fiedler, H. Ullrich (eds.), *Information als Wirtschaftsgut*, Cologne 1997, pp. 93–107 et seq.; H. Zech, *Information als Schutzgegenstand*, 2012, p. 46 et seq.

This has the potential of a basic paradigm shift from the principle of free use of information to the principle of protection of information. If drafting IP rights is about finding the right balance between incentives and access, taking into account the information/semantics level would suggest that the introduction of data rights would have serious consequences. Moreover, an unprecedented problem of the overlap between a new data right and traditional IP, such as copyright, trademark, patent, or database rights, would emerge. Due to the broadness of a data right, any delineation would be difficult to implement.

4.3 Main problems

In light of these more specific proposals, it is time to elaborate on the third counterargument mentioned above, which seems to be the most compelling one against creating new data rights: specification and allocation.

4.3.1 Allocation problem

To use the car example again, it is worth having a closer look at who the new data right should be allocated to.[46] If it is the generator of data, we would still have the choice between different candidates: the producer of the software or data collection device, the producer of the car, the owner of the car, or the driver. All of them could be said to have some interest in data. If you put emphasis on who caused the generation or storage of data from an organizational or economic point of view,[47] which basically refers to investment, it is still not clear whether this would be the owner of the car or the manufacturer. The proposal to distinguish different types of data as to the allocation according to who is responsible for the pertinent act does not appear to be practically feasible.[48] This problem becomes even more obscure when one looks at recordings of data concerning function and resource consumption within smart analytics in networked production sites.[49] A service provider may record data in a production site with his

---

46 G. Hornung, T. Goeble, *"Data Ownership" im vernetzten Automobil...*, pp. 265–266 et seq.
47 H. Zech, Information als Schutzgegenstand..., p. 431.
48 K. Boesche, D. Rataj, *Zivil- und datenschutzrechtliche Zuordnung von Daten vernetzter Elektronkraftfahrzeuge, Begleit- und Wirkungsforschung Schaufenster Elektromobilität (BuW) Ergebnispapier 21*, 2016, p. 41 et seq., propose a different allocation for data concerning the state of the car, the battery, of an electric car, the behavior of the driver and external data like infotainment, and information on service points.
49 F. Bräutigam, P. Klindt, *Digitalisierte Wirtschaft/Industrie 4.0, Expert Opinion 2015*, p. 25, http://bdi.eu/media/themenfelder/digitalisierung/downloads/20151117_Digitalisierte_Wirtschaft_Industrie_40_Gutachten_der_Noerr_LLP.pdf (visited April 20, 2018).

own tools, which are of value to him as well as to the owner of the factory. From an organizational point of view, the service provider or the factory owner may be considered to be the data generator.

In a network of production sites, also other companies along the chain will have an interest in and use for data. Another criterion for the first allocation of rights stemming from economics would be that, in the presence of transaction costs that impede the trade of the right, the right should first be allocated to the person presumed to make the most efficient use of data or who values them most.[50] However, the implementation of this criterion would meet unsurmountable barriers. With different kind of data produced, it might be necessary to determine an efficient allocation for each set of data separately. Moreover, in a networked environment, it will be very difficult to evaluate the relative benefit of data to different stakeholders in the network. For instance, the producer of a car will have an interest in data generated at any stage of the production cycle, be it production times of single components, be it storage time of a distribution partner. This seems to me to be a strong argument against establishing exclusive rights in data. Establishing joint ownership[51] does not seem to be feasible from a practical point of view as well as in the context of the conflicting interests of the stakeholders.

4.3.2 Specification problem

Another problem, even more severe, relates to the issue of specification. For IP protection, the subject matter has to be sufficiently specified to function properly as the subject of exclusive rights. For instance, in copyright, information is (only) protected to the extent it is connected with individuality or creativity as a qualifying criterion. Moreover, general ideas will not be protected, nor will scientific methods for which a need to keep them free from protection has been acknowledged. The protection of data would, at least, result in an unqualified indirect protection of information. It could only be qualified by having recourse to the semantic level.

Moreover, data are just an abstract concept to be distinguished from its physical embodiment. According to the common ISO definition, they can be

---

50 R. Coase, *The Problem of Social Cost*, Journal of Law and Economics 1960, vol. 3, pp. 1, 18; A. Kronman, *Wealth Maximization as a Normative Principle*, Journal of Legal Studies 1980, 9, pp. 227, 240–241.
51 L. Specht, *Ausschließlichkeitsrechte an Daten, Notwendigkeit, Schutzumfang, Alternativen*, Computer und Recht, 2016, pp. 288, 295.

regarded as "a reinterpretable representation of information ... in a formalized manner suitable for communication, interpretation, or processing."[52] In fact, data are the state of information during processing, storage, and communication.[53] If one takes data as the protected subject matter, one would in fact protect that part of the communication process where information is represented in the form of data. Data protection law works differently because it covers only person-related information embodied in data and thus, in effect, has recourse to the semantic level when defining the subject matter, even if data are within the scope of protection.

A serious problem also arises with the fact that in virtualized infrastructures physical control over data is almost impossible (with the cloud as a paradigm). This would make the enforcement of data rights extremely difficult. In practice, increasingly recourse is had to end-to-end encryption on a very low technical level, at best in memory chips, thus denying anybody access to the information included.[54] If this is the way to go, the question will be raised of whether this technological protection itself needs a legal framework to preserve a proper balance of information protection and access, as we have already experienced in the InfoSoc Directive on a different level. Already, the issue is emerging of whether there should be a general right of access to information held privately.[55]

5 Perspectives

The analysis suggests that the case for a new exclusive right has not been made yet.[56] There are severe theoretical and practical impediments to establishing a new exclusive right in industrial data. Moreover, such a right has the potential to limit access to data. There are still two opposite positions: one that perceives establishment of such a right to bring more efficiency and transparency into

---

52 ISO/IEC 2382-1 (1993).
53 This becomes clearer even when one looks at the German Industry Norm DIN 44300: "entities from signs (an element ... out of an total number of objects agreed upon to display information ... and every copy ... of such an element) or continuous functions which because of known or assumed agreement constitute information, mostly for the purpose of processing and as a result thereof" (translated).
54 P. Hoppen, *Sicherung von Eigentumsrechten an Daten*, Computer und Recht 2015, pp. 802, 805.
55 *Digital Single Market strategy for Europe*, COM (2015) 192 final, at 4.1..
56 A. Kerber, *A New (Intellectual) Property Right for Non-Personal Data? An Economic Analysis*, Gewerblicher Rechtsschutz und Urheberrecht, Internationaler Teil, 2016, p. 989 et seq.

the market, and the other, which considers such a right as an impediment to innovation, which would be best served by an unlimited flow of data within a policy of open data and open innovation.[57] More interdisciplinary research is needed before we can make informed decisions on the introduction of such an exclusive right.

The evaluation is difficult also because data covers various and very different kinds of information and is such a broad concept that no comprehensive assessment of interests can be made as a basis for a uniform right on data.[58] One option to consider is to look at specific markets and identify those where market failures occur and then look for the best instruments for regulation. Also, the distinction between raw data and processed data as well as between sensored and machine-generated data may be relevant here.

Another approach could be to distinguish between B2B and B2C. In B2B, the reliance on the existing legal framework in combination with contracts and organizational measures seems to be sufficient from the present perspective ("private ordering"). In B2C, intransparency could be reduced by implementing and refining the existing consumer protection instruments in contract law.[59] Moreover, the focus of consumer protection may remain with the data protection rules.

To keep the market structure competitive, another important issue will be the application of cartel and competition law under the conditions of the developing digital economy. Here, the collection and trading of data is emerging as an important factor of its own.[60] Developing competition law should be part of the more general issue of securing access to information.

The European Commission is still in the process of consultations but in general seems to favor the approach of the free flow of data. This seems to be the right way to move forward. The Communication on Standardisation is based

---

57 G. Hornung, T. Goeble, *"Data Ownership" im vernetzten Automobil*, Computer und Recht, 2015, pp. 265–272.
58 M. Becker, *Rechte an Industrial Data und DSM-Strategie*, GRUR Newsletter 01/2016, p. 7.
59 G. Hornung, T. Goeble, *"Data Ownership" im vernetzten Automobil*,... pp. 265–271.
60 C. Argenton, J. Prüfer, *Search Engine Competition with Network Externalities*, Journal of Competition Law & Economics, 2012, p. 73; *Monopolkommission*, Competition policy: The challenge of digital markets, Special Report No. 68, 2015, n. 109, p. 453 et seqq.; T. Körber, *Ist Wissen Marktmacht? Überlegungen zum Verhältnis von Datenschutz,* "Datenmacht" und Kartellrecht, Neue Zeitschrift für Kartellrecht 2016, vol. 7, p. 303–310 (part 1) and vol. 8 (part 2, pp. 348–355).

on the objective of an open data concept ("IoT ecosystems").[61] The Commission Communication on "Building a European Data Economy" of January 2017 discusses the introduction of a data producer's right in the form of a right in rem or a purely defensive set of rights closer to the protection of know-how. In addition, a right of access to privately held data is envisaged, which could favor certain public interests.[62]

However, the "if" and "how" of such a regulatory intervention are not ready to be determined. Further economic research is needed to identify if and where market failures exist and which positive or negative consequences would result from regulatory activities.[63] The Commission appears to approach this task diligently and stresses the need for further consultations and research efforts. The Communication is quite vague as a result. In any case, it is a step forward, which paves the way for further discussions needed.

---

61 SWD(2016) 110/2, p. 4. M. Becker, *Rechte an Industrial Data und DSM-Strategie*, GRUR Newsletter 01/2016, pp. 7, 11.
62 Cf. Commission Staff Working Document on the free flow of data and emerging issues of the European data economy, SWD (2017) 2 final of 10th January 2017, p. 32 et seq.
63 C. Kerber, *A New (Intellectual) Property Right for Non-Personal Data? An Economic Analysis*, GRUR Int. 2016, p. 989.

Edward Carter

Big Data, Criminal Jurisdiction, and Transnational Crime: How the Long Arm of the Law Reaches across National Borders*

Historically, jurisdiction was seldom a serious issue in criminal prosecutions. Consequently, the subject of criminal jurisdiction was long a sleepy backwater of criminal law. Two phenomena, i.e., the development of the Internet and a worldwide surge in terrorist activity, have conspired to transform that backwater into an important and developing area of criminal law. The advent of Big Data greatly increased the speed and extent of these developments:

> We are witnessing a competitive arms race for data (as opposed to more privacy) — the race to connect the 'data' bucket with the 'money' bucket by many tech firms and investors. Big Data is playing a pivotal role in many companies' strategic decision-making. More companies are adopting data-driven business models and strategies to obtain and sustain a competitive 'data-advantage' over rivals.[1]

Big Data and the Internet are revolutionizing both communications and the manner in which business is conducted. At the same, time the Internet, aided by Big Data, has revolutionized crime by providing new ways to commit traditional crimes as well as giving rise to new types of crimes that are unique to cyberspace and spawned the term "cybercrime" as the label that is commonly applied to both traditional crimes committed with the use of the Internet and those new crimes unique to cyberspace.[2] Important for this article is the fact that the Internet allows perpetrators of cybercrime to commit their crimes from thousands of miles away and across multiple national borders with a keystroke or tap on a computer screen. Almost concomitant has been the dramatic increase in terrorist activity across the globe. That activity is usually facilitated through use

---

* The views expressed in this article are those of the author and do not necessarily reflect the views of the Attorney General of Illinois
1 M. Stucke, A. Grunes, *Big Data and Competition Policy*, Oxford 2016.
2 While a more correct and precise use of the term "cybercrime" is to apply it solely to offenses which can only be committed in cyberspace, this article uses the term as it commonly, if less precisely used: to refer both to traditional crimes committed using computers and to crimes that can only be committed in cyberspace.

of the Big Data and the Internet and, as with cybercrime, a large percentage of terrorist crime as well as its precursor crimes are committed transnationally. The result is that after the identification of the perpetrator, one of the most important, if not the paramount issue, in many cybercrime and terrorist prosecutions is jurisdiction.

In addition to revolutionizing how business is conducted, the Internet has also broadened the subject of judicial risk: from a subject whose primary focus was on evaluating the risk of civil exposure to one whose focus includes, or should include, as an important component evaluating the risk that through the use of email or the internet a business may inadvertently subject itself to the criminal jurisdiction of and prosecution by a foreign sovereign. Because the principles of criminal jurisdiction differ from the law of personal jurisdiction in civil cases,[3] recognizing and evaluating jurisdictional risk poses a particular challenge to both in-house and outside counsel who are familiar with issues relating to long-arm jurisdiction in civil cases but seldom if ever have had to deal with issues of criminal jurisdiction. A particular danger for such practitioners is to assume, incorrectly, that the principles of civil jurisdiction apply to criminal prosecutions.[4]

The risk that a business may inadvertently subject itself to the criminal jurisdiction of a foreign sovereign is heightened by the fact that in the criminal justice system of certain sovereigns a defendant in a criminal case need not be aware of the facts that establish the sovereign's criminal jurisdiction over him.[5] That risk is further heightened in the case of highly technical offenses created in regulatory statutes, the possible violation of which a business may have never considered simply because the business made no affirmative decision to do business in the sovereign's territory and is unaware of the jurisdictional facts which will subject it to a sovereign's criminal jurisdiction. In the case of the United States, that risk is compounded because, like the federal government, states can apply their criminal laws extraterritorially,[6] thereby exposing offshore businesses and business people to the risk of prosecution at either the state or federal level, or both.

This article examines how a sovereign acquires criminal jurisdiction over a person or entity such that in the event the sovereign decides to prosecute, a legally valid verdict can be obtained through the resulting proceeding.

---

3   *United States v. Hayes*, 99 F. Supp.3d 409, 423 n. 4 (S.D. N.Y. 2015).
4   *Ibidem* (principles of jurisdiction in civil cases have no application in criminal prosecutions).
5   *United States v. Manuel*, 371 F. Supp.2d 404, 409 (S.D.N.Y. 2005).
6   *Buffo v. Graddick*, 742 F2d 592 (11th Cir. 1984).

In criminal law, jurisdiction has two elements: a substantive element and a procedural element, both of which must be proven before a legally valid verdict can be rendered. Section 1 of this article examines the substantive element of criminal jurisdiction and Section 2 examines the procedural element.

1 The substantive element of criminal jurisdiction

Substantive criminal jurisdiction, which is usually called "legislative jurisdiction," refers to the power of a sovereign to apply its law to prescribe or regulate conduct.[7] In transnational cases, legislative jurisdiction is the most frequently litigated jurisdictional issue. A sovereign can exercise legislative jurisdiction under either: 1.1) principles of customary international law or 1.2) the sovereign's own domestic law.

1.1 Legislative jurisdiction under principles of customary international law

In the vast majority of criminal prosecutions, if legislative jurisdiction is an issue, a sovereign will usually rely on one of the principles of customary international law for the jurisdictional basis. Whether and the extent to which a sovereign can exercise the jurisdictional power which customary international law recognizes a sovereign as possessing is a question answered by reference to the sovereign's own domestic law. For example, while customary international law recognizes a number of different principles under any one of which a sovereign may exercise legislative jurisdiction, a sovereign's domestic law may only allow it to exercise legislative jurisdiction under one of those principles or a sovereign's law may, as to certain offenses, allow it to exercise jurisdiction under several or all of those principles, but as to all other offenses defined in the sovereign's law allow it to exercise legislative jurisdiction under only one or none of those principles.

Customary international law recognizes five principles of criminal jurisdiction under any one of which a sovereign can exercise legislative jurisdiction.[8] Those principles can be classified as: 1.1.1) non-territorial principles and 1.1.2) territorial principles.

---

7   *Restatement (Third) of Foreign Relations Law of the U.S.*, §401 (1987).
8   *United States v. Rodriguez*, 182 F. Supp. 479 (S.D. Cal. 1961).

1.1.1 Non-territorial principles of legislative jurisdiction

The non-territorial principles of legislative jurisdiction use as their basis or nexus for exercising legislative jurisdiction either the nationality of the perpetrator, the nationality of the victim, the nature of the victim, or the nature of the crime. Because those principles do not use the connection of the crime to the sovereign's territory for their jurisdictional nexus, they allow a sovereign to exercise legislative jurisdiction without regard to where the crime was committed and thereby allow a sovereign to exercise legislative jurisdiction extraterritorially.

Customary international law recognizes a number of non-territorial principles under which a sovereign may exercise extraterritorial legislative jurisdiction. This section examines those non-territorially-based principles and because the extent to which a sovereign can exercise and has exercised extraterritorial jurisdiction is determined by reference to the sovereign's domestic law, it also examines how courts in the United States determine if a criminal statute is to be given extraterritorial effect.

1.1.1.1 The non-territorial principles of legislative jurisdiction recognized by customary international law

Customary international law recognizes four non-territorial principles of legislative jurisdiction. Those four principles are: i) the protective principle; ii) the nationality principle; iii) the passive personality principle; and iv) the universal principle.

i. The Protective Principle
   Of the four principles, the protective principle is the one most relevant to the world of Big Data in which conduct remote from a sovereign's borders can easily adversely affect both the sovereign and its agents at home and abroad. Under the protective principle, a sovereign is allowed to exercise legislative jurisdiction over conduct that occurs wholly outside of the sovereign's borders when that conduct has the potential to adversely affect the sovereign's security,[9] a governmental function of the sovereign,[10] or the sovereign's personnel when acting in their official capacity outside of the sovereign's borders.[11] So, for example, under that principle, a sovereign can exercise legislative jurisdiction over a person outside of the sovereign's territory who, not being one of

---

9   *United States v. Zehe*, 601 F. Supp. 196 (D. Mass. 1985).
10 *United States v. Pizzarusso*, 388 F.2d 8 (2nd Cir. 1968).
11 *United States v. Siddiqui*, 699 F.3d 690, 701 (2nd Cir. 2012).

the sovereign's citizens, engages in espionage against the sovereign.[12] Under that principle, a sovereign can also exercise legislative jurisdiction over a person who while outside of the sovereign's territory and not one of the sovereign's citizens counterfeits official documents of the sovereign,[13] makes false statements to the sovereign agents,[14] or conspires to kill the sovereign's agents while those agents are working in their official capacity outside of the sovereign's territory.[15]

ii. The Nationality Principle
The nationality principle allows a sovereign to exercise legislative jurisdiction over the conduct of the sovereign's own nationals while they are outside of their sovereign's territory.[16] The exercise of legislative jurisdiction under the nationality principle is permissible under American law,[17] but the United States is one of the least aggressive of its proponents.[18] The United States and some western European nations have used this principle to apply their criminal laws to their own citizens when those citizens engage in conduct while within the territory of a foreign sovereign which is criminal under the laws of both the foreign sovereign and the citizen's own sovereign, but which for a variety of different reasons the foreign sovereign tolerates or is unable to prosecute. The nationality principle is usually often used to prosecute crimes such as bribery and sexual misconduct with minors that are committed by a sovereign's citizens while those citizens are within the territory of another sovereign.

iii. The Passive Personality Principle
The passive personality principle allows a sovereign to exercise legislative jurisdiction over foreign nationals who commit crimes against the sovereign's nationals while the sovereign's nationals are outside of the sovereign's territory.[19] That principle has little application to cybercrime and poses no

---

12 *Zehe*, p. 601 F. Supp. 196.
13 *Hanks v. State*, 13 Tex. App. 289 (1882) (counterfeiting title certificates to land in Texas).
14 *United States v. Rodriguez*, 182 F. Supp. 479 (S.D. Cal. 1961) (false statements made in U.S. embassy to obtain a visa).
15 *Siddiqui*, p. 699 F.3d 701.
16 *Skiriotes v. Florida*, 313 U.S. 69 (1941); *State ex. rel. Chandler v. Wisconsin*, 16 Wis. 398 (1863).
17 *Blackmer v. United States*, 284 U.S. 421 (1932).
18 G. Watson, *Offenders Abroad: The Case for Nationality Based Jurisdiction*, 17 Yale J. Intl. L., Winter 1992, pp. 41–42.
19 *United States v. Rezaq*, 134 F3d 1121 (D.C. Cir. 1998); *United States v. Roberts*, 1 F. Supp.2d 601 (E.D. La. 1998).

jurisdictional risk to businesses, but is often used by a sovereign to prosecute perpetrators of terrorist acts against the sovereign's citizens while outside of the sovereign's territory.
iv. The Universal Principle
The fourth of the non-territorially based principles of legislative jurisdiction is the universal principle. There is no generally agreed upon definition of universal jurisdiction in customary international law, but the essence of the principle embodies the power of a sovereign to apply its law outside of the sovereign's territory, without regard to the nationality of the victim, and without regard to the nationality of the perpetrator.[20] Thus, unlike all other forms of international jurisdiction, universal jurisdiction is not premised on notions of sovereignty or state consent and in fact is intended to override them.[21]

Historically, the only crime subject to universal jurisdiction was piracy.[22] Since at least the early 1600s, any nation could try any pirates it caught regardless of the pirates' nationality or where on the high seas they were apprehended.[23] After World War II, nations sought to extend universal jurisdiction to other kinds of crimes such as war crimes and genocide on the rationale that piracy was subject to universal jurisdiction because of its heinousness,[24] and because war crimes and genocide are also heinous, the perpetrators of those crimes are also subject to universal jurisdiction.[25] That extension is controversial[26] and the heinousness rationale deployed in service of that extension is dubious at best.

The extension is controversial for two reasons: 1) It is controversial because, at least with respect to acts of state, it has the potential for sparking interstate conflict and for being used as a tool of interstate conflict[27] and 2) It is controversial because it empowers a foreign sovereign to use its criminal justice system

---

20 R. Hesenov, *Universal Jurisdiction for International Crimes—A Case Study*, Eur. J. Crim. Policy Res, 2013, 19, p. 275.
21 E. Kontorovich, *The Piracy Analogy: Modern Universal Jurisdiction's Hollow Foundation*, 45 Harv. Int. L. J., Winter 2004, pp. 183–184.
22 *Ibidem*.
23 *Ibidem*, p. 190.
24 *Ibidem*, p. 185.
25 *Ibidem*.
26 H. Kissinger, *The Pitfalls of Universal Jurisdiction*, Foreign Affairs, July/August 2001, p. 86.
27 Madeline H. Morris, *Universal Jurisdiction in a Divided World: Conference Remarks*, 35 New Eng. L. Rev., 2001, pp. 337–340.

to defeat internal political settlements of another sovereign relating to human rights abuses within the territory of that other sovereign.[28]

At the same time, the heinousness rationale is problematical because, as one commentator has observed, piracy is not a particularly heinous crime[29]—it is little more than robbery at sea[30] and in the past nations, including the United States, were recognized as having the power to authorize it through the issuance letters of marque and reprisal.[31] Thus, to the extent the piracy/heinousness rationale is used to extend universal jurisdiction to apply to crimes other than piracy, that extension is of questionable legality at best.[32] Consequently, even to the extent that cybercrime may be used to promote transnational terrorism, whether those cybercrimes can be prosecuted under the universal principle is open to serious question.

1.1.1.2 How American courts determine if a criminal statute is to be given extraterritorial effect

A sovereign's domestic law may allow the sovereign to exercise legislative jurisdiction extraterritorially, but as to any specific offense that simply raises the question: as to that offense to what extent has the sovereign chosen to exercise legislative jurisdiction extraterritorially? The domestic law of the United States, for example, allows it to exercise legislative jurisdiction extraterritorially,[33] but as

---

28 H. Kissinger, *The Pitfalls of Universal Jurisdiction,…*, p. 86.
29 E. Kontorovich, *The Piracy Analogy: Modern Universal Jurisdiction's Hollow Foundation*, …, p. 210.
30 *Ibidem*, p. 191.
31 The U.S. Constitution specifically give Congress the power "to grant Letters of Marque and Reprisal." *U.S. Const.*, Art. I, Sec. 8, cl. 11.
32 Some commentators have suggested that universal jurisdiction exists for piracy offenses because those offenses are committed outside the territorial jurisdiction of any nation. Kontorovich, *The Piracy Analogy: Modern Universal Jurisdiction's Hollow Foundation*, at 190. That rationale overlooks or ignores the fact that the ship attacked by pirates is flagged by a particular sovereign and hence within that sovereign's flag jurisdiction (See discussion of flag jurisdiction *infra*.) and that those on board the victim ship are nationals of some sovereign and hence within that sovereign's passive personality jurisdiction. *Ibidem*. Some commentators cite slave trading as an offense for which universal jurisdiction existed before the post-World War II era. *Ibidem*, p. 192. No state practice supports universal jurisdiction over slave trading. *Ibidem*, p. 193. Instead, international treaties on slave trading delegated jurisdiction whereby the several signatory nations conveyed to one another the right to exercise some of their jurisdiction powers with respect to those offenses.
33 *United States v. Ayesh*, 702 F.3d 163, 166 (4th Cir. 2012).

to any specific offense the question is to what extent has the United States chosen to do so?

In the United States, that question is answered as a matter of statutory construction.[34] The easy case is when Congress states that a particular criminal statute is to have extraterritorial effect. When a criminal statute is jurisdictionally silent, such as the statute that defines the offense of Securities Fraud,[35] there is a presumption that the statute is not intended to apply extraterritorially.[36] That presumption, however, does not apply when: 1) the criminal statute defines an offense as one committed against the government or government personnel; 2) the failure to extend the scope of the criminal statute extraterritorially will result in adverse effects within the United States; or 3) the conduct regulated by the statute occurs within the United States.[37]

In the United States, if a crime is within the legislative jurisdiction of the federal government, the offender need not be aware of the facts that establish that jurisdiction over him.[38] Thus, the fact that a defendant is not aware that his conduct or the results of his conduct would subject him to the legislative jurisdiction of the United States is irrelevant to deciding whether the United States can exercise that jurisdiction over him.

1.1.2 The territorial principle of jurisdiction

The fifth jurisdictional principle recognized by customary international law is the territorial principle. That principle relies on the connection of a crime to the sovereign's territory as the basis for exercising legislative jurisdiction. The territorial principle has two distinct aspects, either one of which can be used by a sovereign as a ground for exercising legislative jurisdiction. The two aspects of the territorial principle are: 1.1.2.1) subjective territorial jurisdiction and 1.1.2.2) objective territorial jurisdiction.

1.1.2.1 Subjective territorial jurisdiction

Under international law, subjective territorial jurisdiction is the primary source of legislative jurisdiction.[39] Subjective territorial jurisdiction recognizes in the

---

34 *Ibidem.*
35 15 USC §78(b).
36 *United States v. Vilar*, 729 F.3d 62, 73 (2nd Cir. 2013).
37 *Ibidem.*
38 *Manuel*, pp. 404–409. The domestic law of the different states within the United States may differ as to the necessity of knowledge of jurisdictional facts.
39 *United States v. Laden*, 92 F. Supp.2d 189, 195 (S.D. N.Y. 2000).

sovereign the power to exercise legislative jurisdiction over the perpetrators of crimes that have situs in the sovereign's territory.[40] Criminal statutes create two different types of offenses: offenses which make a specific act criminal and offenses which make a specific result criminal. That distinction is important in determining where a crime has its situs and thus whether the sovereign can exercise legislative jurisdiction over the crime's perpetrator under the subjective aspect of the territorial principle.

In the case of condemned act criminal statutes, the situs of the crime is the place where the condemned act is performed. For example, the offense of forgery which, in conjunction with other elements, *inter alia*, makes it a crime to make a document which purports to be made by one who did not make it.[41] The condemned act in that statute is the making of the spurious document. Under that definition of the offense, the situs of the forgery offense, i.e., the place where the condemned act was performed, is the place where the spurious document is made.

To determine whether a condemned act crime was committed within the sovereign's subjective territorial jurisdiction, i.e., within the sovereign's territory, it is critical to look at and understand the act which the applicable statute makes criminal. The offense of Wire Fraud[42] provides an example of why it is critical to understand what act a criminal statute condemns and how the statute operates before a conclusion can be reached about the situs of that crime.

The offense of Wire Fraud proscribes the use of the telecommunication systems of the United States to further a scheme whereby one intends to defraud another of property.[43] As the offense is defined, it includes as its elements the existence of a scheme to defraud someone of money or property and the use of a radio signal or the wires for the purpose of furthering the scheme.[44] The *actus reus* of the offense, i.e., the physical act that the offense condemns and the performance of which completes the crime, is the use of radio signals or the wires to further the scheme.[45]

In the Big Data environment, telecommunication systems are routinely used in fraud schemes, so one might well expect the Wire Fraud statute to apply

---

40 *Ibidem*.
41 See, e.g., the Illinois offense of Forgery, 720 ILCS 5/17-3.
42 18 USC 1343.
43 *United States v. Trapilo*, 130 F.3d 547, 552 (2nd Cir. 1997).
44 *Fountain v. United States*, 357 F.3d 250 (2nd Cir. 2005).
45 *United States v. Poliak*, 823 F.2d 371, 372 (9th Cir. 1987); *United States v. Molinaro*, 11 F.3d 853, 859 (9th Cir. 1993).

extraterritorially. The statute, however, is silent as to its extraterritorial application, and though there is some disagreement among federal circuits, the Wire Fraud statute is generally held not to apply extraterritorially.[46] In those federal circuits where the Wire Fraud statute is held not to apply extraterritorially, that territorial limitation does not, however, preclude application of the statute to foreign nationals who hatch their schemes wholly overseas even when those schemes are not designed to cause effects in the United States.

In *United States v. Hayes*,[47] Hayes and another defendant named Darin were neither U.S. citizens nor residents. The two were employed by USB Bank as short term interest Yen traders. Darin traded from USB locations in Singapore, Tokyo, and Zurich. Hayes traded from a USB location in Tokyo. The federal criminal complaint filed in U.S. District Court in the Southern District of New York charged the two with conspiracy to commit Wire Fraud by manipulating the London Interbank Offered Rate (LIBOR) for Yen. The manipulated LIBOR that resulted from their actions was published to servers around the world, including in New York. Though the criminal complaint did not allege that either defendant traded Yen LIBOR swaps with counter parties in New York, confirmations for certain trades with a New York counter party affected by the manipulated rates were electronically routed from UBS' overseas offices to servers located in the Southern District of New York.

Darin moved to dismiss the charge. In his motion, Darin noted first that the Wire Fraud statute did not apply extraterritorially and then noted that he was a Swiss citizen living outside the United States who was charged with conspiring to manipulate a foreign financial benchmark for a foreign currency while working for a foreign bank in a foreign country.[48] Based on that, Darin argued his prosecution involved an unauthorized extraterritorial application of the conspiracy and Wire Fraud statutes and for that reason the charges should be dismissed.[49]

Agreeing with Darin that the Wire Fraud statute did not apply extraterritorially, the court nonetheless rejected Darin's argument, holding that the statute was not being applied extraterritorially. The court pointed out that in the offense of Wire Fraud it is the use of the domestic wires that is criminal and the allegation in the criminal complaint that the defendants caused the manipulated LIBOR to be published to servers in the United States and that United States wires were used

---

46 *Hayes*, pp. 409–419.
47 99 F. Supp.3d 409 (S.D. N.Y. 2015).
48 *Ibidem*, p. 412.
49 *Ibidem*, p. 419.

to memorialize trades affected by the manipulated rate meant that the conduct criminalized by the statute occurred in the United States.[50]

The court also rejected Darin's argument as to the conspiracy charge, noting that there is jurisdiction to try conspirators who have never entered the United States where the conspiracy was directed to violation of the United States' law within the United States.[51]

In the case of condemned result criminal statutes, the situs of the crime is the place where the result occurs. The offense of murder is an example of a condemned result offense. That offense condemns causing the death of another and when the death is caused in conjunction with the other elements of the offense the crime of murder has occurred.[52] Under that definition, the act that brings about the death, for example, shoot or stabbing, is not condemned, instead it is the result of the act that is condemned and thus, the situs of the crime is the place where the condemned result occurs.[53] For example, if X is on a British ship on the high seas and shoots at Y who is on an American ship also on the high seas and Y dies from the gun shot, the criminal act takes effect on the American ship and under the subjective aspect of the territorial principle of jurisdiction X is subject to criminal prosecution by the United States.[54]

1.1.2.2 Objective territorial jurisdiction

Under the objective aspect of territorial jurisdiction, a sovereign is recognized as having the power to exercise legislative jurisdiction to make criminal conduct performed completely outside of the sovereign's territory when the condemned act is intended to produce and does produce a substantial detrimental effect within the sovereign's borders.[55]

Under the Big Data regime, one would expect objective territorial jurisdiction to expand, and it does appear to be evolving in a number of different ways, all of which have the effect of broadening the principle. Some courts state the detrimental effect prong of the principle disjunctively instead of conjunctively, saying that the principle can be used when the crime is intended to produce *or* does produce substantial detrimental effects in the United States.[56] That formulation

---

50 *Ibidem*, p. 421.
51 *Ibidem*, p. 425.
52 See, e.g., the Illinois offense of First Degree Murder, 720 ILCS 5/9-1(a).
53 *United States v. Davis*, 25 Fed Cases 786 (C.C.D. Mass. 1837).
54 *Ibidem*.
55 *Strassheim v. Daily*, 221 U.S. 280 (1911).
56 *United States v. Hayes*, 653 F.2d 8 (1st Cir. 1981).

of the principle is usually used with the crime of conspiracy, where it is held that it is the aim of the conspiracy and not its effects that determines jurisdiction.[57] Thus, in conspiracy cases, for example, no act in furtherance of the conspiracy need be performed in the United States and the effects of the conspiracy need not yet have been felt there as long as the object of the conspiracy would produce detrimental effects there.[58]

Other courts have jettisoned the intent element of the detrimental effects prong of the principle and held that the objective territorial principle can be used when the crime merely produces substantial detrimental effects within the United States.[59]

Courts are quite liberal in deciding what, under the detrimental effects prong of the principle, constitutes a detrimental effect. Thus, courts have found the following effects to be sufficiently detrimental to satisfy the requirements of the detrimental effects prong: the cost and necessity of psychological counseling for an American victim of sexual assault on the high seas combined with cost of an American criminal investigation of the crime;[60] increased prices for paper in the United States caused by a price fixing agreement reached in a foreign country;[61] theft of data from a bank located in the United States.[62]

1.1.2.3 Flag jurisdiction

Ships flagged by a sovereign are considered to be part of the sovereign's territory while on the high seas, essentially being treated like islands which belong to the sovereign. As such, flag jurisdiction is a species of territorial jurisdiction. In admiralty jurisdiction, high seas include seas and the waters that are tributary to them to the extent they are navigable.[63] Thus, for purposes of admiralty jurisdiction "high seas" includes rivers within the jurisdiction of a sovereign other than that of the sovereign under whose flag a vessel sails.[64]

---

57 *United States v. Al Kassar*, 660 F.3d 108, 119 (2nd Cir. 2011).
58 *United States v. Baker*, 609 F.2d 134, 138 (5th Cir. 1980); *United States v. Arra*, 630 F.2d 836 (1st Cir. 1980).
59 *United States v. Rogers*, 1 F. Supp.2d 601 (E.D. La. 1998); *Baker*, 609 F.2d, p. 138.
60 *Rogers*, 1 F. Supp.2d, p. 601.
61 *United States v. Nippon Paper Industries*, 109 F.3d 1 (1st Cir. 1997).
62 *United States v. Ivanov*, 175 F. Supp.2d 367 (D. Conn. 2001).
63 *United States v. Flores*, 289 U.S. 137 (1933).
64 *Ibidem*.

1.1.3 Limitations on the exercise of legislative jurisdiction

Both customary international law and, at least with respect to certain sovereigns, the sovereign's own domestic law place limits on the exercise of legislative jurisdiction.

1.1.3.1 Limitation imposed by customary international law

Customary international law imposes an important limitation on the ability of a sovereign to exercise legislative jurisdiction under any of the five principles examined above. Assuming one of the bases for exercising legislative jurisdiction under customary international law exists, a sovereign cannot exercise legislative jurisdiction with respect to a person or activity having a connection with another sovereign when it would be unreasonable to do so.[65] Customary international law looks at various factors considered to be relevant to determining reasonableness. In general, no single factor is determinative, but there are two clear cases in which it is not unreasonable for a sovereign to exercise legislative jurisdiction over a person or activity having a connection to another sovereign: 1) when the condemned conduct or condemned result is universally condemned[66] or 2) when the condemned conduct or condemned result is condemned by all sovereigns that could assert jurisdiction and the sovereign exercising legislative jurisdiction is one of those sovereigns.[67]

1.1.3.2 Limitations imposed by domestic law

In the United States, the due process clause of the Fifth Amendment also limits the extent to which the United States can exercise legislative jurisdiction extraterritorially[68] and the Fourteenth Amendment's due process clause imposes the same limits on a state's power to exercise extraterritorial legislative jurisdiction. The Fifth Amendment due process clause requires that before legislative jurisdiction can be exercised extraterritorially that there be a sufficient nexus between the defendant and the United States[69] or, in the case of the extraterritorial exercise of legislative jurisdiction by an American state, between the defendant and the exercising state. Such a nexus exists when the aim of a defendant's

---

65 *United States v. Vasquez-Velasco*, 15 F.3d 833 (9th Cir. 1994).
66 *Ibidem.*
67 *Nippon Paper Industries*, 109 F.3d, p. 1.
68 *United States v. Mostafa*, 2013 WL 4714158 (S.D.N.Y. 2013).
69 *Ibidem.*

activity is to cause harm inside the United States or to citizens or interests of the United States.[70]

The due process clause also embodies a fair notice requirement, which requires that criminal statutes be written clearly enough that a defendant be able to understand that his conduct or the result of his conduct is proscribed.[71] The purpose of the fair notice requirement is to give a person fair notice that his contemplated conduct or the results of his conduct is forbidden by the statute.[72] The fair notice requirement does not, however, require that the jurisdictional statute be clear enough for the defendant to understand that he could be subject to prosecution in the United States.[73]

1.2 Exercise of legislative jurisdiction solely under domestic law

Customary international law is not the only source of a sovereign's legislative jurisdiction. A sovereign may under its domestic law exercise legislative jurisdiction in a way which overrides international law.[74] Thus, for example, in the United States, Congress has the power to override international law if it chooses[75] and the principles of customary international law do not limit Congress's power to exercise legislative jurisdiction extraterritorially.[76] Consequently, a sovereign can ignore the limits of legislative jurisdiction imposed by customary international law and apply its criminal statutes to persons whose extraterritorial conduct would not, under those principles, subject them to a sovereign's legislative jurisdiction and still obtain a valid verdict under its domestic law.[77] Before an American court will construe an American statute as having extraterritorial application, the court will try to construe it as being consistent with one or more of the principles of jurisdiction recognized by international law.[78] If after examining the applicable statute a court concludes that its exercise of extraterritorial jurisdiction violates international law, the court will nonetheless give it extraterritorial effect if there is an explicit Congressional directive to do so.[79]

---

70 *United States v. Al Kassar*, 660 F.3d 108 (2nd Cir. 2011).
71 *Bouie v. City of Columbia*, 378 U.S. 347 (1964).
72 *United States v. Chestman*, 947 F.2d 551, 564 (2nd Cir. 1991).
73 *Al Kassar*, 660 F.3d, p. 108.
74 *Laden*, 92 F. Supp.2d, p. 196.
75 *Ibidem*.
76 *United States v. Yunis*, 924 F.2d 1086, 1091 (D.C. Cir. 1991).
77 *Ibidem*.
78 *Laden*, 92 F. Supp.2d, p. 196.
79 *Ibidem*.

2 The procedural aspect of criminal jurisdiction

Procedural criminal jurisdiction, which is usually called adjudicative jurisdiction, refers to the power of a sovereign's court to subject a person to its judicial process.[80] Assuming a sovereign has the power to exercise legislative jurisdiction either under the principles of customary international law or its own domestic law, before the tribunal that will determine guilt or innocence and impose punishment can proceed against the defendant, the tribunal must have personal jurisdiction over him. Personal jurisdiction is called *in personam* jurisdiction. A tribunal cannot proceed against a defendant if it does not have *in personam* jurisdiction over him. Generally, whether a tribunal has *in personam* jurisdiction over a defendant is determined by the domestic law of the prosecuting sovereign.

In the United States, a tribunal obtains *in personam* jurisdiction over a defendant in a criminal case when the defendant first appears before it. *In personam* jurisdiction is acquired either when the defendant voluntarily appears before the court, such as when he surrenders in court before being arrested, or when he is brought involuntarily before the court, such as when he has been arrested by the sovereign's law enforcement agents.

One area of recurring controversy is whether a tribunal obtains *in personam* jurisdiction over a defendant who is brought before it through extralegal actions of either the sovereign's law enforcement agents or of its private citizens. In the United States, those controversies have usually arisen when American law enforcement agents have ignored an existing extradition treaty, entered a foreign country, and, without following procedures set out in the treaty, arrested the defendant there and forcibly brought him back to the United States for trial. Within the United States, that controversy has arisen as well when law enforcement agents of one state have gone to another state, arrested a defendant, and, without going through the interstate extradition process required under the U.S. Constitution, taken him back to their state for trial.

With respect to extralegal arrests in and transfers from a foreign country to the United States, the U.S. Supreme Court as well as state supreme courts have consistently held that in the absence of a provision in the relevant treaty that expressly prohibits extralegal arrests, an American court acquires *in personam* jurisdiction notwithstanding the extralegal conduct of either American law enforcement agents[81] or private citizens.[82] The U.S. Supreme Court has also held

---

80 *Restatement (Third) of Foreign Relations Law of the United States*, §401(b)-(c) (1987).
81 *Kasi v. Virginia*, 256 Va. 407 (1998).
82 *Ker v. Illinois*, 119 U.S. (1886).

that a state court acquires *in personam* jurisdiction over a defendant notwithstanding the fact that the state's law enforcement agents made an extralegal arrest in another state and ignored interstate extradition procedures when bringing him back to the prosecuting state.[83]

Once a court obtains *in personam* jurisdiction over a defendant, that jurisdiction continues even if the defendant subsequently flees the jurisdiction or simply fails to appear for trial. Consequently, a defendant who flees after *in personam* jurisdiction is acquired over him may be tried *in absentia*.[84]

---

83 *Frisbie v. Collins*, 342 U.S. 519 (1952).
84 In the United States before a defendant can be placed on trial *in absentia* the prosecutor must establish to the court that the defendant was admonished that if he fails to appear for trial he may be tried *in absentia*. As a matter of course defendants are given that admonishment by the judge when the defendant makes his first appearance in court and prosecutors note in their file the date and the name of the judge who gave them.

Arkadiusz Lach

Identity Theft in the European Union: Do We Need Harmonization?

1 Introduction

Identity theft is without a doubt one of the most widely discussed and commonly recognized crimes related to the development of new technology and information systems. That is why it is sometimes called a crime of the Digital or Information Age.[1] Of course, it is not a new crime as the history of crime is full of examples of criminals pretending to be someone else. However, the development of information technology and the Internet has given identity theft a new life. The processing of information in an electronic form and the verification of identity based on knowledge, not possession, certainly make the gathering of personal data and their subsequent unlawful use much easier.

Identity theft may have many forms and may be easily committed even by persons with limited technical skills and knowledge. The scale of the crime in some countries and the impact on the victims and economies of the Member States raise a question of whether the phenomenon should be harmonized in the European Union (EU). In this chapter, three questions will be answered:

- Should we criminalize identity theft at all?
- What should be the limits of criminalization?
- Should the elements of crime and punishment be harmonized in the EU?

2 Definition of identity theft

Before we move to the issue of harmonization, some terminology issues must be addressed as there is no one common definition of identity theft, which causes problems in researching and discussing this phenomenon. Let us look at a few proposed definitions as they occur in various documents and countries.

---

1   D. Solove, *The Legal Construction of Identity Theft*, Symposium Digital Cops in a Virtual Environment, Yale Law School, March 26–28 2004, p. 6.

B. – J. Koops and R. Leenes define identity theft as "fraud or another unlawful activity where the identity of an existing person is used as a target or principal tool without the person's consent."[2]

The EU Fraud Prevention Expert Group used the definition created by the United Kingdom Fraud Prevention Service (Cifas), according to which "[i]dentity theft is generally defined as the misappropriation of the identity (such as the name, date of birth, current address or previous addresses) of another person, without their knowledge or consent. These identity details are then used to obtain goods and services in that person's name."[3]

The Australian Law Reform Commission concludes that identity theft is "the illicit assumption of a pre-existing identity of a living or deceased person, or of an artificial legal entity such as a corporation."[4]

In a communication from the European Commission from 2007, we may find a very general definition of identity theft, which is described as "the use of personal identifying information, e.g. a credit card number, as an instrument to commit other crimes."[5]

Some authors prefer to use the term "identity fraud," indicating that the object (identification data) is still in possession of the rightful owner.[6] According to B. De Vries, J. Tigchelaar, and T. van der Linden, "[i]dentity fraud is to obtain, to possess or to create intentionally, (and) (unlawfully or without consent) false means of identification in order to commit unlawful behaviour, or to have the intention to commit unlawful behaviour."[7] On the other hand, others use the expression "identity fraud" only in relation to crimes committed with intent to gain a benefit or avoid an obligation,[8] i.e., crimes against property. From this

---

2 B. J. Koops, R. Leenes, *Identity Theft, Identity Fraud and/or Identity-related Crime*, Datenschutz und Datensicherheit 30 (2006) 9, p. 556.
3 http://ec.europa.eu/internal_market/fpeg/identity-theft_en.htm, last access 01.02.2018.
4 Australian Law Reform Commission, *For Your Information: Australian Privacy Law and Practice*, ALRC Report 108, May 2008, http://www.alrc.gov.au/sites/default/files/pdfs/108_vol1.pdf, p. 474, last access 01.02.2018.
5 Commission of the European Communities, *Communication from the Commission to the European Parliament, the Council and the Committee of the Regions. Towards a general policy on the fight against cyber crime*, Brussels 22.05.2007, COM (2007) 267 final, p. 8.
6 B. De Vries, J. Tigchelaar and T. van der Linden, *Describing Identity Fraud: Towards a Common Definition*, Scripted, vol. 5, nr 3, December 2008, p. 489.
7 *Ibidem*, p. 495.
8 Australian Law Reform Commission, *For…*, p. 474.

point of view, using the identity of another person for illegal purposes may not in every case be described as an identity fraud. One other reason to distinguish the category of identity fraud is that the perpetrator may use a fake identity to hide his real identity while committing a crime, in which case personal data are not used.

In a United Nations study, it was observed that the terms "identity theft" and "identity fraud" were not used consistently and they do not describe the problem fully.[9] Therefore "[i]n the present report, scenarios in which genuine identity information or documents are actually taken or misappropriated are described as 'identity theft', while scenarios in which identities were used to deceive others are referred to as 'identity fraud'. Cases in which identities or related information were simply fabricated are not analogous to either fraud or theft, although some States considered those to be identity fraud based on subsequent misuse of the identities."[10]

A slightly different approach was taken by the EU in the directive on attacks against information systems,[11] where the phenomenon of identity theft was characterized as "misusing the personal data of another person, with the aim of gaining the trust of a third party, thereby causing prejudice to the rightful identity owner" (article 9 (5)). It should also be mentioned that article 10 (3) of the proposal[12] addressed "concealing the real identity of the perpetrator and causing prejudice to the rightful identity owner."

The most convincing definition of identity theft indicates three elements of the act:

a. use of personal data of another person,
b. without authorization,
c. with intent to commit illegal act or in a way that may cause harm to the person whose data are used.

---

9   Economic and Social Council, *Report of the second meeting of the Intergovernmental Expert Group to Prepare a Study on Fraud and the Criminal Misuse and Falsification of Identity*, E/CN.15/2007/8/Add.3, 31 January 2007, p. 5.
10 *Ibidem*.
11 Directive 2013/40/EU of the European Parliament and of the Council of 12 August 2013 on attacks against information systems and replacing Council Framework Decision 2005/222/JHA, OJ L 218 from 14.8.2013.
12 European Commission, Proposal for a directive of the European Parliament and of the Council on attacks against information systems and repealing Council Framework Decision 2005/222/JHA, COM (2010) 517 final.

It is also useful to distinguish identity theft from identity fraud and identity crime. Identity fraud is the kind of fraud whereby a false identity was used to commit a crime. In most countries, one of the elements of fraud is deceit. Deceit may mean misleading someone as to the identity of the perpetrator of the act. He or she may use both the real identity of someone else or the fictional identity of a non-existing person. Therefore, on one hand, the notion of identity fraud is broader than the notion of identity theft because it also encompasses fictional identities. On the other hand, identity fraud is limited only to the cases when an attack is directed against property, leaving aside such behaviors as the creation of false profiles on social networking sites in order to harass the data subject.

It should also be mentioned that identity crime is the broadest term used to describe criminal acts whereby false identity is a means to committing a crime or the target of criminal activity. This encompasses both identity theft and identity fraud.

3 Modus operandi of the perpetrators

Identity theft may take on many forms. Some examples include the following:

a. Creation of profiles on Social Networking Sites pretending to be profiles of other people, e.g., a colleague from school, work, former partner, public person.
b. Obtaining a bank loan in the name of somebody else.
c. Credit card fraud. This is one of the most common examples of identity theft, whereby the perpetrator, without authorization, uses the credit card data of another person to pay for goods or services.
d. Identity theft connected with car plates. The offender uses stolen or duplicated car plates while driving, which may subject the rightful owner of the car to criminal or civil responsibility for traffic offenses or claims related to outstanding gas or parking bills
e. Unauthorized access to computer systems, whereby the perpetrator uses someone else's login data in order to gain access to a computer system (and potentially commit other crimes).
f. Stating someone else's personal data while caught in the act, which may result in the arrest and prosecution of an innocent person.
g. Phishing, whereby someone uses the data of another person or organization trying to get the data of a third party (e.g., login data, personal identification number, personal data). This is usually done in preparation for another act of identity theft during which the fraudulently obtained data are used.

These are only some examples of identity theft. There are various forms of this phenomenon and their number is growing, especially with the development of technology and electronic services.

4 Reasons for criminalization

Statistics show that identity theft is a quite frequently committed act. A Eurobarometer survey from 2012 shows that 8% of respondents were victims of identity theft.[13] Other statistics quote an even higher of 13%.[14] Another study estimates that 2% of the EU population are affected by identity theft, with an average loss of around 2,500 euro, which amounts to a total of 20 billion euro in the EU.[15]

In the United Kingdom, the statistics of Cifas for 2014 quote 114,000 identity frauds, which constitutes 41% of all instances of fraud recorded through Cifas in 2014.[16]

In France, 4.2% of respondents declared that they had been victims of identity theft in the past ten years, although the statistics are contested and the number of identity thefts reported per year to the police is said to be between 6,000 and 10,000.[17]

Looking at the statistics, one must also have in mind that this is not the full picture of the scale of identity theft. Many acts are not reported due to their trivial character (e.g., phishing), lack of hope of identifying the perpetrator, lack of a relevant criminal provision to hold the perpetrator responsible, potential

---

13 http://europa.eu/rapid/press-release_IP-12-751_en.htm?locale=en, last access 01.02.2018.
14 V. Marinho, *Analysis of the Cybercrime with Spatial Econometrics in the European Union Countries* in: M. M. Cruz-Cuhna, I. M. Portela, *Handbook of Research on Digital Crime, Cyberspace Security and Information Assurance*, IGI Global 2014, p. 489.
15 European Commission, *Study for an Impact Assessment on a proposal for a new legal framework on identity theft, Center for Evaluation and Strategy Services*, 11 December 2012, http://ec.europa.eu/dgs/home-affairs/e-library/documents/policies/organized-crime-and-human-trafficking/cybercrime/docs/final_report_identity_theft_11_december_2012_en.pdf, p. 172, last access 01.02.2018.
16 Cifas, Fraudscape. *UK fraud trends*, http://www.cifas.org.uk/secure/contentPORT/uploads/documents/External%20-%20Fraudscape%20main%20report%20for%20website.pdf, p. 4, last access 01.02.2018.
17 http://ethique-tic.fr/2012/labasedestitreselectroniquesdesecurite/ampleur-de-lusurpation-didentite/, last access 01.12.2015.

harm connected with the disclosure of the offense (e.g., impact on clients, position of the person), and other factors.

While assessing the damage caused by identity theft, we must take into consideration both the damage caused to primary victims (persons whose identities were misused) and secondary victims (persons or collective bodies who were defrauded or victimized in other ways by the perpetrator's using the personal data of the primary victim). It must be also underlined that identity theft causes both financial and nonfinancial damages (e.g., stress, fear, loss of reputation).[18] The significance of the latter should not be underestimated.

Therefore, the need for criminalization could arise from the scale of the phenomenon and the damage caused both directly and indirectly. Often, direct damage is not the most important or visible (e.g., small amount of money lost) but the subsequent effects (e.g., loss of reputation, criminal records for crimes not committed) may have much more severe consequences for the victim.

One important factor is evidentiary obstacles in proving other, usually more serious crimes, e.g., fraud. Another is preventing other crimes. In certain countries, such as the United States, the range of criminalization is very wide and a person is criminally responsible even for the possession of personal data of another person with the intention of committing a crime. This gives law enforcement agencies power to act at an early stage of a criminal activity.

The need for criminalization may be also related to the positive obligations of states under article 8 of the European Convention on Human Rights. As the European Court observed in the case of KU v. Finland, "[a]lthough this case is seen in domestic law terms as one of malicious misrepresentation, the Court would prefer to highlight these particular aspects of the notion of private life, having regard to the potential threat to the applicant's physical and mental welfare brought about by the impugned situation and to his vulnerability in view of his young age."[19] Then, stressing the positive obligation of the parties under article 8 of the Convention, the Court indicated that "[t]hese obligations may involve the adoption of measures designed to secure respect for private life even in the sphere of the relations of individuals between themselves. There are different ways of ensuring respect for private life and the nature of the State's obligation will depend on the particular aspect of private life that is at issue. While the choice of the means to secure compliance with Article 8 in the sphere of protection against acts of individuals is, in principle, within the State's margin of

---

18 See European Commission, *Study*..., pp. 55–78.
19 KU v Finland, judgment from 2 December 2008, application 2872/02, par. 41.

appreciation, effective deterrence against grave acts, where fundamental values and essential aspects of private life are at stake, requires efficient criminal-law provisions."[20]

Therefore, the need for protecting the privacy of the citizens guaranteed by article 8 may also encompass criminal law provisions and their effective enforcement. Of course, the circumstances of the KU case were special, as central to it was the issue of protecting a minor against potential approaches by pedophiles. Therefore, it was treated very seriously by the European Court of Human Rights. However, one must bear in mind that in many cases of identity theft the effects may be very serious to the victim and the damage irreparable.

It is, however, necessary to pose a question of whether criminalization is the best means for preventing and fighting identity theft. Before the answer is given, it must be observed that criminal law and criminal procedure are reactive steps and they are taken when the abuse has already happened. Additionally, the damage is usually irreparable. Also, seeing as the detection rate is low and there are serious evidentiary problems with proving guilt (especially in the case of private prosecutions), it is difficult to rely too much on criminal law. However, the existence of criminal law provisions may be regarded as general deterrence and would enable victims (natural persons) to protect their rights. In many countries, only secondary victims (e.g., victims of fraud or other subsequent criminal activities) may act as parties in a criminal procedure while primary victims are only heard as witnesses. In the case of the criminalization of identity theft, both types of witnesses may participate in criminal proceedings. The latter facts provide sufficient grounds for criminalization.

Nevertheless, we must be aware that only a complex program of prevention, detection, prosecution, and minimization of the effects of identity crime may visibly reduce the problem. The most important issue is the education of citizens in terms of how to protect their personal data and not disclose them to potential offenders. In the age of Social Networking Sites and other electronic services, it is very important to raise the awareness of the users, starting from primary schools. Any such program should also encompass making people alert to different signs of identity theft in order to detect misuse as early as possible. Another potential threat is the use of publicly available electronic databases, from which the perpetrator may easily obtain personal data for unlawful purposes.[21] In the context

---

20 *Ibidem*, par. 43.
21 The American example of the publication of court judgments without anonymization is case in point. In Poland, problems could be caused by the Central Register and

of business, services, and government agencies, it is also important to ensure that the systems of verification of identity are as secure as possible. One important solution is also a data breach notification duty, introduced first to electronic communication law[22] and now generally in relation to personal data databases.[23]

To sum up the above arguments, it could be said that the criminalization of identity theft as a legal phenomenon taking on different forms is necessary.

5 Models of criminalization

After supporting the rationale of criminalization, we shall now look at how it could be done. There are different ways of criminalizing identity theft. The models of criminalization may be distinguished with the use different criteria.

The first criterion is the number of legal provisions criminalizing identity theft. Gercke distinguishes between the single provision approach and multi provision approach.[24] I would describe these models as concentrated and dispersed criminalization. It is hard to imagine that all relevant issues could be dealt with by a single provision, but there could be one, single most important regulation in place. In the case of dispersed criminalization, there are several criminal law provisions without a core regulation intended for identity theft.[25]

Information on Economic Activity (Centralna Ewidencja i Informacja o Działalności Gospodarczej: CEIDG) and Electronic Land Register (Elektroniczne Księgi Wieczyste: EKW). The first contains information on persons running their own firms, while the second contains information on land owners.

22 Article 4 of the Directive 2002/58/EC of the European Parliament and of the Council of 12 July 2002 concerning the processing of personal data and the protection of privacy in the electronic communications sector (Directive on privacy and electronic communications), OJ UE L 201 from 31.7.2002.

23 Articles 33 and 34 of the Regulation (EU) 2016/679 of 27 April 2016 on the protection of natural persons with regard to the processing of personal data and on the free movement of such data, and repealing Directive 95/46/EC (General Data Protection Regulation), OJ UE L 119 from 4.5.2016.

24 M. Gercke, *Internet-related identity theft*, Strasbourg, 22 November 2007, pp. 20–21.

25 In my research on the criminalization of identity theft, I found in the Polish criminal legislation about 20 criminal law provisions which may be used for the prosecution of offenders. Beside the core provision, they concern such crimes as defamation, fraud, use of forged documents, use of someone else's ID card, use of someone else's digital signature, perjury, serving prison sentence for someone else, unauthorized access to information systems, stating false personal data to law enforcement authorities. See A. Lach, *Karnoprawna reakcja na zjawisko kradzieży tożsamości (Penal law reaction on identity theft phenomenon)*, Warszawa 2015, pp. 105–139.

It must be observed that identity crime has become a crime *per se* and, consequently, States are moving toward concentrated criminalization. It is also important to determine if identity theft is treated in a more traditional way as something directed against property or alternatively reputation or more as something directed against privacy and personal data.

The second criterion is the scope of the crime. It is possible to criminalize a wide range of behaviors or concentrate on the main illicit activity. In the first situation, criminalization may apply to such behaviors as unauthorized possession of personal data, gathering of personal data with intent to commit a crime, selling personal data, or transfer of personal data for criminal activity. A good example of a very wide criminalization is the statutory provision introduced in 1996 in Arizona, according to which "[a] person commits taking the identity of another person or entity if the person knowingly takes, purchases, manufactures, records, possesses or uses any personal identifying information or entity identifying information of another person or entity, including a real or fictitious person or entity, without the consent of that other person or entity, with the intent to obtain or use the other person's or entity's identity for any unlawful purpose or to cause loss to a person or entity whether or not the person or entity actually suffers any economic loss as a result of the offense, or with the intent to obtain or continue employment."[26] Statutory language with a similarly wide scope of criminalization was introduced at the federal level by the *Identity Theft and Assumption Deterrence Act 1998*.[27] As one may observe, criminalization also encompasses the unauthorized possession of personal data with intent to commit a crime.

If criminalization applies to preparatory acts, attempt, and the core crime, we may speak about complex criminalization. This issue depends largely on the particular national criminal law. For example in Poland, according to the general part of criminal law, an attempt is always punished but preparation is punished only if there is a specific provision.

The next issue is that of whether identity theft should be a material or formal crime. In the first situation, a crime is committed when the activity has a result (damage, harm, increased risk). In the case of formal crime, no result of criminal activity is required to prove a crime. In the context of the idea of criminalization at an early stage and evidentiary problems in the case of material crimes, the formal character of the crime should be supported.

---

26 Arizona Revised Statutes, 13 – 2008.
27 18 USC § 1028 (7).

The last question is whether criminalization of identity theft should protect only natural persons or also legal persons or other collective bodies. The specificity of identity theft and the links with personal data and privacy are the reasons for which protection should be limited to living natural persons. Collective bodies such as companies may be protected, e.g., by regulations against unfair competition or defamation.

6 Criminalization of identity theft in chosen EU Member States

Criminalization of identity theft is quite different across member states compared to, e.g., theft or fraud. To show the differences, four countries were chosen: Belgium, England, France, and Poland.

In Belgium, there are no explicit statutory provisions concerning identity theft. The prosecution of this offense takes place in accordance with the statutory provisions criminalizing fraud, unauthorized processing of personal data, etc.

In England, the most relevant statutory provision is in the Fraud Act 2006. Under section 2 of the act (Fraud by false representation):

1. A person is in breach of this section if he or she—
    a. dishonestly makes a false representation, and
    b. intends, by making the representation—
        i. to make a gain for himself or another, or
        ii. to cause loss to another or to expose another to a risk of loss.
2. A representation is false if—
    a. it is untrue or misleading, and
    b. the person making it knows that it is, or might be, untrue or misleading.

Under section 1 (3) of the act, a person who is guilty of fraud is liable—

   a. on summary conviction, to imprisonment for a term not exceeding 12 months or to a fine not exceeding the statutory maximum (or to both);
   b. on conviction on indictment, to imprisonment for a term not exceeding 10 years or to a fine (or to both).

In France, a new provision was introduced to the criminal code in 2011.[28] Article 226-4-1 criminalizes the "act of usurping the identity of an individual or the act of using one piece or several pieces of data of any kind enabling his/her identification with a view to disturb his/her tranquility or that of others, or with a view

---

28 Loi n 2011-267 du 14 mars 2011.

to prejudice her honor or reputation." The crime is punishable by up to 1 year of deprivation of liberty and a fine of up to 15,000 euros.

In Poland, a new provision aimed at the criminalization of identity theft was introduced in 2011.[29] Under article 190a § 2 of the criminal code, anyone impersonating another person and using the image or personal data of that person with intent to cause financial or moral harm to them faces up to 3 years of deprivation of liberty. If the act results in an attempted suicide of the victim, the punishment ranges from 1 to 10 years of deprivation of liberty. The crime is prosecuted on the motion of the victim.

One of the weaknesses of the Polish regulation is the requirement of intent. Proving intent causes problems because the perpetrator may argue that he or she was acting out of fun or for personal gain, and not in order to cause moral or personal harm to the person whose personal data were used (although under the circumstances of the case it was inevitable or probable). On the other hand, the provision is not limited to financial harm and the lawmaker placed the provision in the same article as stalking.

The short presentation of the four legal systems leads to the following conclusions:

a. Not in all Member States is identity theft criminalized as crime per se.
b. There are different legal goods protected by the legislation: property, personal data, privacy, honor (reputation), and freedom from harassment.
c. Identity theft is usually treated as a formal crime.
d. There is usually the requirement of the intent connected with the use of personal data.
e. Identity theft criminalization protects natural persons.
f. The penalties are various.

The criminalization of identity theft should be effected within certain limits but at the same time be efficient. Regulations similar to those adopted in US federal law and in Arizona would be certainly too far-reaching. In the context of identity crime, criminal law should also protect the privacy of the person, not only property. Therefore, identity theft should not be construed as a material crime, as this would make the prosecution of offenders very difficult. The protection of personal data limits criminalization to situations where the victim is a living natural person. Also, penalties for identity theft should be adequate. Three to five

---

29 Ustawa z dnia 25 lutego 2011 r. o zmianie ustawy – Kodeks karny, Dz. U. Nr 72, poz. 381.

years of deprivation of liberty as the upper limit seems to be reasonable. Such a penalty would make it possible to issue an extradition request or a European arrest warrant. Additionally, in the case of a European arrest warrant, a penalty of at least three years of deprivation of liberty for an identity theft which is a computer crime could enable the authorities to use the exception to the double criminality requirement provided in article 2 (2) of the framework decision on the European arrest warrant.[30]

7 To harmonize or not?

The legal base for the harmonization of criminal law provisions can be found in article 83 of the Treaty on the Functioning of the European Union,[31] according to which:

> 1. The European Parliament and the Council may, by means of directives adopted in accordance with the ordinary legislative procedure, establish minimum rules concerning the definition of criminal offences and sanctions in the areas of particularly serious crime with a cross-border dimension resulting from the nature or impact of such offences or from a special need to combat them on a common basis. These areas of crime are the following: terrorism, trafficking in human beings and sexual exploitation of women and children, illicit drug trafficking, illicit arms trafficking, money laundering, corruption, counterfeiting of means of payment, computer crime and organised crime.
> On the basis of developments in crime, the Council may adopt a decision identifying other areas of crime that meet the criteria specified in this paragraph. It shall act unanimously after obtaining the consent of the European Parliament.
> 2. If the approximation of criminal laws and regulations of the Member States proves essential to ensure the effective implementation of a Union policy in an area which has been subject to harmonisation measures, directives may establish minimum rules with regard to the definition of criminal offences and sanctions in the area concerned. (…)

As one may observe, cybercrime was *expressis verbis* mentioned as one potential area for harmonization. Certainly, identity theft is often committed through information systems, although it could be also committed in other ways, which

---

30 Council Framework Decision of 13 June 2002 on the European arrest warrant and the surrender procedures between Member States, OJ L 190 from 18.07.2002.
31 Consolidated versions of the Treaty on European Union and the Treaty on the Functioning of the European Union—Consolidated version of the Treaty on the Functioning of the European Union, *Official Journal C 326 from 26.10.2012.*

do not constitute a cybercrime. The potential EU instrument should, therefore, focus on these types of identity theft which are concerned with information technology, leaving aside other forms of the crime.

Another question is if there are other factors warranting harmonization, such as the cross-border character or a particular seriousness of the crime. The first issue could be answered in the negative. Identity theft does not seem to have a considerable international dimension. Rather, it is a crime committed within borders, except for identity fraud, which is punished as a form of fraud, and illegal access to computer systems, which was harmonized already with reference to identity theft by the 2013 directive. Besides, criminals may often operate from countries outside EU. As regards the term "particularly serious crime," doubts may arise as to whether identity theft has such a character. On one hand, this crime does not seem to be as serious as terrorism, drug trafficking, or human trafficking. On the other, given the scale, potential harm for victims, and impact on the economy, the crime could be regarded as serious.

The harmonization of identity theft regulations was recognized as an issue which should be further investigated by the Commission, which in 2007 expressed the view that, "[i]n most Member States, a criminal would most likely be prosecuted for the fraud, or another potential crime, rather than for the identity theft; the former being considered a more serious crime. Identity theft as such is not criminalised across all Member States. It is often easier to prove the crime of identity theft than that of fraud, so that EU law enforcement cooperation would be better served were identity theft criminalised in all Member States."[32]

Two different positions were taken in the comparative reports prepared for the European Commission in the course of the further analysis of the problem as announced in the Communication from 2007. The first report, from 2011,[33] "does not directly support that there is a universal need for EU action, since no instances have been identified where an act of identity theft as described in Chapters 1 and 2 of this report could not be punished at the national level." The authors of the report indicated nonlegal responses as the priority for any policy

---

32 Commission of the European Communities, *Communication from the Commission to the European Parliament, the Council and the Committee of the Regions. Towards a general policy on the fight against cyber crime*, Brussels 22.05.2007, COM (2007) 267 final, p. 8.

33 N. Robinson and others, *Comparative Study on Legislative and Non Legislative Measures to Combat Identity Theft and Identity Related Crime: Final Report*, Rand Europe, June 2011, p. 114.

approach and cautioned that any new legislation may overlap with that already existing, especially concerning fraud and forgery.[34]

However, in the 2012 report,[35] it was indicated that there is "[a] need for a Directive including a common definition of identity theft as a framework for further initiatives to combat identity theft in the future, including possible criminalization is seen as useful by many of those consulted in the framework of the present study. Such an approach would demonstrate that the Commission is responding to the need for action to tackle the growing problem of identity theft with measures that are practical and add value to what Member States are already doing." The main arguments were that complex regulations concerning identity theft and identity-related crime would address the legislative gap in relation to identity theft for primary victims and could introduce nonlegislative measures in the form of an online platform and a network of contact points.[36]

The directive on attacks against information systems from 2013 deals with the issue of identity theft in article 9, sub. 5, declaring that "Member States shall take the necessary measures to ensure that when the offenses referred to in Articles 4 and 5 [Illegal system and data interference-AL] are committed by misusing the personal data of another person, with the aim of gaining the trust of a third party, thereby causing prejudice to the rightful identity owner, this may, in accordance with national law, be regarded as aggravating circumstances, unless those circumstances are already covered by another offense, punishable under national law." In par. 14 of the preamble, we may find a rather ambiguous statement that "[s]etting up effective measures against identity theft and other identity-related offences constitutes another important element of an integrated approach against cybercrime. Any need for Union action against this type of criminal behaviour could also be considered in the context of evaluating the need for a comprehensive horizontal Union instrument."

The directive deals with the issue of identity theft only in the context of cyberattacks and the Member States are only obliged to treat the misuses of identity as an aggravating circumstance. Not requiring at the same time any specific increased punishment means that this obligation could be fulfilled without a change in the legislation, as usually, when deciding on the penalty, the court is taking into consideration all circumstances of the case and may treat the unauthorized use of personal data and potential harm for the data subject

---

34 *Ibidem*, p. 119.
35 European Commission, *Study*..., p. 177.
36 *Ibidem*.

as circumstances warranting an increased penalty. Separate criminalization of identity theft is not required but such criminalization is regarded as an alternative to introducing aggravating circumstance. This concept might prove ineffective in countries which recognize a separate crime of identity theft but punish it relatively less severely than attacks against information systems. If these actions are treated as one act and one penalty is imposed on the offender, the punishment will not necessarily be higher.

A more far-reaching provision was included in the proposal for the directive.[37] According to article 10 (3), Member States shall take necessary measures to ensure that the offenses referred to in articles 3 to 6 (illegal access to information systems, illegal system interference, illegal data interference, illegal interception) are punishable by criminal penalties of a maximum term of imprisonment of at least five years when committed by concealing the real identity of the perpetrator and causing prejudice to the rightful identity owner. This provision was, however, changed on grounds that a complex instrument for criminalization of identity theft is needed and "[s]etting up effective measures against identity theft and other identity-related offenses constitutes another important element of an integrated approach against cybercrime. Any need for Union action against this type of criminal behaviour could also be considered in the context of evaluating the need for a comprehensive horizontal Union instrument."[38]

The issue of harmonization at the EU level is, therefore, still open. Under the assumption that harmonization is decided upon, the question is what other measures beside criminalization should be included. Those which should be taken under consideration are setting up a database of identity theft crimes in the EU, which could help in investigations and protection of the victims, and creating a network of contact points in the Member States able to deal quickly with requests to assist from law enforcement authorities. Statistical data on identity theft should also be gathered and analyzed in order to introduce the most relevant policy of preventing and fighting this crime.

---

37 European Commission, Proposal for a directive of the European Parliament and of the Council on attacks against information systems and repealing Council Framework Decision 2005/222/JHA, COM (2010) 517 final.

38 Council of the European Union, Proposal for a Directive of the European Parliament and of the Council on Attacks against Information Systems, replacing Council Framework Decision 2005/222/JHA – General approach, 11566/11.

8 Conclusions

Identity theft is a widely recognized behavior which may cause significant damage to individuals and to a state's economy. The criminalization of this phenomenon is not the most important or effective solution, as criminal law is reactive. As it was shown in the article, the criminalization of the behavior in question may take different forms. This analysis and other studies show that identity theft is at least to some extent criminalized in all Member States, even if there are no specific statutory provisions on it.

There is an obligation to criminalize identity theft under article 8 of the European Convention on Human Rights on the parties to the Convention, which was emphasized in the case of KU v Finland. However, there are doubts as to whether criminalization is necessary at the EU level, given the character of the crime and already existing criminalization in the Member States. In the Treaty on Functioning of the European Union there is a legal base for harmonization if identity theft is in the form of a cybercrime (other types of crimes listed in article 82 are of minor importance in relation to the issueof criminalization of identity theft), which may be a starting point for future initiatives. Such initiatives have already been undertaken in the directive on the attacks against information systems.

If the harmonization is decided upon by the EU, the following main points should be taken into consideration:

- Identity theft should be treated as a crime against privacy, not against property or economy.
- Proving intent should not be required, and so potential harm should be enough for prosecution.
- Identity theft should also be criminalized in the case of moral harm, and not only financial harm.
- There should be a wide margin for implementation by the Member States, given the existing regulations and specific features of criminal law in the Member States.

Joanna Marszałek

Identity Theft in the United States: A Different Perspective?

1 Definition

Identity theft, which is the fastest-growing criminal activity in the United States,[1] is a crime where personal data are wrongfully obtained and used by another person.[2] It may take the form of stealing such data as the Social Security Number, bank account information, or even illegal acquisition of a patient's medical record. The main reason for using someone's identity is gaining financial advantages or obtaining a loan or other benefits, but sometimes it is a kind of a "non-profit" crime, for example, when it takes on the form of stealing somebody's social networking service account to post embarrassing contents. The crime is strictly connected with the term "identity fraud," which occurs when the fraudster uses the stolen identity to obtain goods or services, for example credit cards or documents such as passports or driver's licenses, to take out loans or open bank accounts.[3] Even though the statistics are not accurate, as a lot of people and businesses simply do not report the crimes to the police, a more disquieting fact is that a big number of people do not even know their data have been stolen; in 2005, it was said that a person's identity was stolen every four seconds.[4] Almost 15 million US residents are victims of this white-collar crime, which causes financial losses to the country of up to $50 billion every year.[5]

The phenomenon was identified as a federal crime by *The Identity Theft and Assumption Deterrence Act of 1998*, which amended 18 U.S.C. § 1028. Until 1998, the crimes which are now defined as identity thefts were classified as "false

---

1 F. Abagnale, *Stealing Your Life: The Ultimate Identity Theft Prevention Plan.*
2 Information from the U.S. Department of Justice: https://www.justice.gov/criminal-fraud/identity-theft/identity-theft-and-identity-fraud, last access: April 9, 2018.
3 http://www.actionfraud.police.uk/fraud_protection/identity_fraud, last access: April 9, 2018.
4 F. Abganale, *Stealing Your Life…*
5 See: *Identity Theft and Scan Prevention Services*, R. Douglas: http://www.identitytheft.info/victims.aspx, last access: April 9, 2018.

personation," which can be described as "the crime of falsely assuming the identity of another to gain a benefit or avoid an expense."[6] The abovementioned Act established the penalties for committing the crime of up to 15 years of imprisonment. What is more, law enforcement agencies, such as the Secret Service and the Federal Bureau of Investigation, were invested with powers of taking actions against this crime. The act also established the Federal Trade Commission (FTC) as a central agency which supports investigation and prosecution by creating the Identity Theft Data Clearinghouse.[7] Because of the rapid expansion of new technologies, 18 U.S.C. § 1028, which previously stated that only the production or possession of false identification documents was prohibited, needed to be amended.[8] Presently, not only the person who produces or possesses such documents shall be punished but also the one who "knowingly transfers, possesses, or uses, without lawful authority, a means of identification of another person" (s.a(7)). The "means of identification" are broadly described in s.d(7) and include:

(A) name, social security number, date of birth, official State- or government-issued driver's license or identification number, alien registration number, government passport number, employer or taxpayer identification number;
(B) unique biometric data, such as a fingerprint, voice print, retina or iris image, or other unique physical representation;
(C) unique electronic identification number, address, or routing code; or
(D) telecommunication identifying information or access device (as defined in section 1029(e)).

As can be seen, in the age of modern technologies, when committing crimes of identity theft is easier than it was even twenty years ago, the legislation needed to be amended, as 18 U.S.C. § 1028 was no longer an effective weapon against identity thieves. As a response to the rapid growth of the phenomenon, the Congress passed the *Identity Theft and Assumption Deterrence Act of 1998* to aid the fight against this crime.

State legislature-wise, it is worth noticing that Arizona was the first U.S. state which identified identity theft as a discrete crime in 1996.[9] The Arizona Criminal

---

6 http://ojp.gov/ovc/pubs/ID_theft/idtheftlaws.html, last access: April 9, 2018.
7 See: the information from the Federal Trade Commission: https://www.ftc.gov/news-events/media-resources/identity-theft-and-data-security, last access: April 9, 2018.
8 B. Finkelstein, *Identity Theft and Assumption Deterrence Act of 1998*, 1999, p. 1.
9 J. Clough, *Principles of Cybercrime*, Cambridge University Press, 2010, p. 208.

Code, § 13-2008, states that "[a] person commits taking the identity of another person or entity if the person knowingly takes, purchases, manufactures, records, possesses or uses any personal identifying information or entity identifying information of another person or entity, including a real or fictitious person or entity, without the consent of that other person or entity, with the intent to obtain or use the other person's or entity's identity for any unlawful purpose or to cause loss to a person or entity whether or not the person or entity actually suffers any economic loss as a result of the offense, or with the intent to obtain or continue employment."[10] As a consequence, many states followed in Arizona's footsteps and passed specific identity theft regulations, which are unique in each state in terms of the definition of the phenomenon, the types which are criminalized, and the treatment of the crime (whether it is a felony or misdemeanor).[11] For example, according to South Dakota legislature, a person commits the crime of identity theft if he or she "without the authorization or permission of another person and with the intent to deceive or defraud obtains, possesses, transfers, uses, attempts to obtain, or records identifying information not lawfully issued for that person's use or accesses or attempts to access the financial resources of that person through the use of identifying information." Identity theft is committed under the circumstances specified by section §22-40-8 of the S.D. Codified Laws and is a Class 6 felony. According to Iowa legislature, "a person commits the offense of identity theft if the person fraudulently uses or attempts to fraudulently use identification information of another person, with the intent to obtain credit, property, services, or other benefit. If the value of the credit, property, or services exceeds one thousand dollars, the person commits a class 'D' felony. If the value of the credit, property, or services does not exceed one thousand dollars, the person commits an aggravated misdemeanor" (Iowa Code §715A-8). It is important to point out that most identity theft prosecutions take place at the state level because of the small amounts of money involved in such cases, which means that they are not pursued by federal prosecutors.[12]

As mentioned above, the statistics are not accurate because many people simply do not report that crime. However, some agencies tried to show the scale

---

10 A. Lach, *Karnoprawna reakcja na zjawisko kradzieży tożsamości*, Lex, Warszawa 2015, p. 71.
11 G. Newman, M. McNally, *Identity theft literature review*, 2005, pp. 63–64.
12 *Ibidem*, p. 64.

of the phenomenon. The Federal Trade Commission reported that, in 2014, out of the 2,582,851 total consumer complaints filed or collected, 332,646 were related to identity theft.[13] On the basis of the statistics which come from the Federal Trade Commission Sentinel Network, Florida was the state most significantly contributing to the nation-wide number of the instances of identity theft as well as identity fraud in 2014: more than 11% of all reported identity theft complaints came from the "Sunshine State." Aside from Florida, the states recording the highest rates of identity theft complaints are Arizona, Nevada, California, Texas, and Georgia.[14]

The public awareness of the scale of this crime is still surprisingly low. What is more, prices at which personal data are sold on the black market are incredibly low: for instance, a Social Security Number can be bought for less than $50 and the driver's license for $90.[15] It means that it can take the victim many years to realize that someone else has been using their name, creating an enormous overdraft on their bank account. Additionally, as new technologies are developing, it is easier to illegally obtain someone's identity and use it for gaining benefits. Frank Abagnale, a professional identity thief, whose life inspired Steven Spielberg's *Catch me if you can* movie, said: "What I did was almost 50 years ago and it's about 4,000 times easier today to con people than when I did it. To forge a cheque 50 years ago, you needed a Heidelberg printed press, you had to be a skilled printer, know how to do colour separations, negatives, type-setting… those presses were 90 feet long and 18 feet high. There was a lot of work involved in creating a cheque. Today, you open a laptop."[16]

Although identity theft is not a new criminal activity, the methods which criminals use *are* new and are getting less complicated, as people share more information via social networking services.[17] What is more alarming is the fact that a thief does not need a lot of information to steal someone's identity: sometimes all they need is a name and a photo. In 2013, a student of the Sukkivan County School District in Sullivan Count, Tenessee, Ira Trey Quesenberry III, used the name and likeness of the principal of the school, Dr. Jubal Yennie, and created a Twitter account in Yennie's name. The tweets shared via this

---

13 *Ibidem*, p. 3.
14 *Ibidem*, p. 9.
15 F. Abagnale, *Stealing Your Life…*
16 http://www.wired.co.uk/article/frank-abagnale, last access: April 9, 2018.
17 J. Velasco, *Does Over-Sharing Leave You Open to the Risk of Identity Theft?* (http://socialnomics.net/2016/01/13/4-case-studies-in-fraud-social-media-and-identity-theft/, last access: April 9, 2018).

account were reported to be of an embarrassing nature and not appropriate for a superintendent.[18] After realizing she was a victim of the identity theft crime, Dr. Yennie contacted the police and the student was arrested. A similar situation was encountered by Sarah Palin, a former Alaska Governor. A person who created a fake Twitter account of Palin's tweeted out an open invitation for a barbecue party at Palin's family home. As can be seen, not only a private person may become an identity theft victim: many public figures and celebrities as well as politicians (notice how many fake social networking services accounts were created for 2016 presidential candidates Hillary Clinton and Donald Trump) are threatened by it. One of the most spectacular identity thefts affected Ben Bernanke, the Federal Reserve Board chairman, who has been issuing warnings about the scale of this phenomenon for years. On 7 August 2008, his wife's purse was stolen while she was sitting at a Starbucks coffee shop. Unfortunately, not only the purse was stolen but also the "perfect combination" of Anna Bernanke's personal data: her Social Security Number, date of birth, home address, and telephone number.[19] A few days later, these data were used for suspicious bank transactions, which were fortunately spotted by Ben Bernanke, and no money was lost as a result.[20]

Identity thieves use varied techniques to obtain identifiable data about individuals. There is no doubt that the most popular one is simply stealing someone's credit card, Social Security Number, or medical record. A common method is also the Internet, for example, hacking into mailboxes or bank account websites as well as stealing someone's Twitter or Facebook account or creating a fake one. However, some techniques are truly outlandish, for example "dumpster diving" and rummaging through rubbish for personal data. It is estimated that more than 80% of personal data collected by identity thieves came from garbage.[21] After paying the bills, many people just discard them to the trash bin, not realizing that they may contain sensitive information such as address, full name, or credit card number. Thieves are constantly on the lookout for such documents

---

18 R. Siciliano, *The Social Media Identity Theft of a School Director Via Twitter* (http://www.huffingtonpost.com/robert-siciliano/highschooler-goes-social-media_b_2550541.html, last access: April 9, 2018).

19 http://www.fightidentitytheft.com/blog/ben-bernanke-identity-theft-victim, last access: April 9, 2018.

20 http://europe.newsweek.com/ben-bernanke-victimized-identity-theft-ring-78773?rm=eu, last access: April 9, 2018.

21 http://www.identitytheftaid.org/types-of-identity-theft/secure-trash/, last access: April 9, 2018.

as well as other pieces of "trash": old credit cards, tax documents, or loan information, and then use the sensitive information which they contain.

Another technique, which nowadays is the easiest way to illegally obtain sensitive information about individuals, is undoubtedly the Internet, IT equipment, and storage media. As mentioned earlier, the quicker the development of technology, the greater the possibility to use it for illegal purposes. As Frank Abagnale wrote in his book *Stealing Your Life*, "[t]he Internet is one of the most versatile research tools a criminal has ever been handed."[22] Regarding this statement, there are also some situations when preventing a data security breach is out of our hands: in 2011, Sony suffered a massive breach in its PlayStation Network and Qriocity services. One of the largest Internet security break-ins, it saw the names, addresses, and possibly credit card data belonging to 77 million user accounts compromised.[23] However, even a regular telephone call may land someone the personal data of an individual, which will then be used against this person. The so-called common-knowledge questioning schemes, whereby the caller requests, for example, account verification, asking questions such as "what is your mother's maiden name" or "what is your account number," may see these data used by the fraudster in the future.

What is more, in the United States, a lot of records, such as phone books, voter registration lists, police reports, military reports, Social Security Administration death certificates, marriage and divorce records, or even boat registration documents, are public and easy to get. All of these records contain sensitive information which can be easily used by criminals. On top of that, people do not realize that in many cases when they are asked to give their Social Security Number, for example during a veterinary appointment, they do not, in fact, have to comply.[24] And if they do, the probability that it will be illicitly used increases. There were also cases reported when the victim sent their personal data as a response to fake job offers, and after a few months realized that their identity had been stolen and used without their knowledge. The important thing is to be aware of what an identity thief may do to obtain our personal data, what kind of techniques they can use, and what the most popular types of this phenomenon are. This information may help us fight this crime and prevent us from becoming an identity theft victim.

---

22 F. Abagnale, *Stealing Your Life*…
23 L. Baker, J. Finkle, *Sony PlayStation Suffers Massive Data Breach* http://www.reuters.com/article/us-sony-stoldendata-idUSTRE73P6WB20110426, last access: April 9, 2018.
24 F. Abagnale, *Stealing Your Life: The Ultimate Identity Theft Prevention Plan*.

2 Types of identity theft

2.1 Financial identity theft

Financial identity theft is the most common and pervasive type of that crime. As already mentioned, each year, identity theft costs the US up to $50 billion in losses and the average loss of money per victim is $3,500.[25] The main aim of financial identity thieves is to gain economic benefits at the expense of the victim. The list of the consequences of that is long but the most popular frauds committed by means of stolen identity are: credit card frauds, investment, checking or saving account frauds, mortgage and loans frauds, and finally tax frauds.[26] The last one occurs when someone's stolen Social Security Number is used to file a tax return claiming a fraudulent refund.[27] This type of fraud is specified by 18 U.S. Code § 286, which states that it is illegal to conspire to defraud the United States with respect to claims as well as 18 U.S. Code § 287, which also states that making or presentment of a claim upon the United States which is known to be false, fictitious or fraudulent is illegal. Many cases show how the identity of an oblivious individual can be easily used to obtain fraudulent tax refunds. The most spectacular one is undoubtedly *409 F.2d 814 Kenneth A. Kercher v United States*, whereby the defendant was charged with the violation of the abovementioned 18 U.S. Code § 287. Kenneth A. Kercher's business was to prepare income tax returns and claim tax refunds. To perform such actions, he needed a signed power of attorney from each taxpayer authorizing him to prepare tax returns. Ten individuals made such an agreement with Kercher. However, the defendant was only authorized to file tax returns in a single year. A year later, Kercher used the personal data of his clients without their authorization and prepared tax returns in their name. The refunds were sent to the addresses controlled by Kercher, as none of the taxpayers had the knowledge about the addresses used in the form filled in by the defendant.[28]

Financial identity theft was also at the center of case *159 F.3d 401 United States v Akintobi and Ani*, when the defendants purchased credit cards which had been stolen from mails. They collected cash advances and made purchases on the cards until the credit limit was reached. They had also opened checking accounts

---

25 See: Identity Theft and Scan Prevention Services, R. Douglas: http://www.identitytheft.info/financial.aspx, last access: April 9, 2018.
26 See: Identity Theft and Scan Prevention Services, R. Douglas: http://www.identitytheft.info/financial.aspx, last access: April 9, 2018.
27 https://www.irs.gov/uac/taxpayer-guide-to-identity-theft, last access: April 9, 2018.
28 *Kenneth A. Kercher v. United States of America.*

in the cardholders' names and finally withdrew the money used to open them, leaving the balance at zero. The defendants were charged with money laundering in violation of § 1956.[29] However, according to the current wording of *The Identity Theft and Assumption Deterrence Act of 1998*, their actions would nowadays be considered in violation of the Act, as they established checking accounts in the names of people who had not authorized them to do it and as they clearly intended to break the law.[30]

2.2 Child identity theft

Identity theft cases among children are becoming more common every year, although it is very hard to determine if the child's identity has been unlawfully used. In many cases, the crime is revealed when the person is old enough to apply for a credit card or a driver's license. The statistics showing the scale of the phenomenon are extensive, but certainly its full extent is not known. The 2012 Child Identity Fraud Report stated that 1 in 40 households with children under the age of 18 had at least one child whose personal data had been targeted by identity thieves.[31]

This type of crime is closely connected with *synthetic identity theft*, which happens when the identity is fully or only partially fabricated, especially by combining a real Social Security Number with the name and date of birth of the individual not connected with the Number.[32] Regarding the Social Security Numbers of children, they are very valuable for criminals as very often no information is associated with them. What is even more terrifying is the fact that the access to children's data is easy as it can be gained through school or tax forms, papers at the doctor's office which are not properly stored, and of course social networking services, where a child posts sensitive information, which, however, he or she does not perceive as such.

As already mentioned, long years may elapse until a parent realizes that their child's identity has been illegally used. However, there are some signs which may indicate that a criminal came into possession of personal data with a view to illegally using them. First of all, when a child receives credit cards, insurance, or other financial offers, it means that his or her data were added to a database of,

---

29 United States of America v. Adedayo Omokayode Akintobi and Olugbenga Olusoji Ani.
30 B. Finkelstein, *Identity Theft and Assumption Deterrence Act of 1998*, 1999, p. 7.
31 http://www.parents.com/kids/safety/tips/what-is-child-identity-theft/, last access: April 9, 2018.
32 L. Britnell, *The Changing Face of Identity Theft*.

for example, a bank. Another warning sign may be a situation whereby a parent wants to open a financial or bank account and the application is rejected because of an unsatisfactory credit history of the child or when it turns out that the child's credit report already exists.[33]

Richard Power of the Carnegie Mellon Cylab reported that, according to the data supplied by AllClear ID, 10.2% of 40,000 children were victims of identity theft. It shows that the scale of the phenomenon is huge and is additionally aggravated by the fact that children as well as their parents are typically unaware of that fact for years and find out about it in a situation when they do not expect it at all.

2.3 Criminal identity theft

Criminal identity theft occurs when a person who is charged or arrested uses someone's identity (their name and other information which can identify a person), which results in a criminal record being established in the name of the person whose identity was stolen.[34] The victim may not even know that a warrant of arrest has been issued under his or her name and can be arrested during a routine traffic control and taken into custody on the strength of that warrant. This happened to Brittany Ossenfort in 2007. The woman decided to find a roommate and after some time she was introduced to Michelle, with whom she decided to share an apartment for more than one year. However, there were numerous signs that should have alerted Brittany. Michelle started to imitate her roommate's style: she got the same hairstyle, got the same tattoo located in the same spot as Brittany's. One day, when Brittany was at work, she was contacted by police officers asking her to bail herself out of jail. At the police station, she realized that her roommate had stolen her identity and had been charged for prostitution, posing as Brittany Ossendorf. Fortunately, the fingerprints confirmed that "the real Brittany" was innocent and that she had become a victim of criminal identity theft. What is more, it turned out that Michelle was a transgendered woman and was finally identified as a Richard Philips.[35]

Also the *Joyce Ann Brown case* shows how stolen identity can be used by a criminal to avoid liability for crimes committed. In 1980, Joyce Ann Brown read

---

33 http://identitytheftnetwork.org/gethelp/i-was-a-child-victim, last access: August 2016.
34 See the information from the California Department of Justice: https://oag.ca.gov/idtheft/criminal, last access: April 9, 2018.
35 http://www.identityguard.com/identity-theft-resources/articles/victims-name-used-in-jail-in-bizarre-identity-theft-case/, last access: August 2016.

in a newspaper that she was a murder suspect. Two days earlier, a fur coat store was robbed by two women, who killed the owner of the store, Rubin Danziger, and then escaped in a rental car. When the abandoned vehicle was found, the police established that the renter was Joyce Ann Brown. Photographs of women who had a record for prostitution were shown to the store owner's wife, who had survived the robbery, and she identified the murderer. The consequences of this case of mistaken identity were serious, as Brown was charged and sentenced to 9 years of imprisonment. In 1989, Texas Criminal Court of Appeals finally quashed her conviction and she was released. In February 1990, the charges were dropped.[36] It shows that the consequences of that type of crime can be really serious and steps should be taken to avoid it.

2.4 Medical identity theft

In 2015, the data of more than 90 million American citizens were stolen due to data breaches at health insurers': CareFirst, BlueCross, BlueShield, Anthem, and Premera.[37] According to the Identity Theft Resource Center, the highest percentage of total hackings of all industries affects the health and medical sector: in 2014, this figure stood at 42.5%.[38] It is estimated that each year almost 250,000 Americans are victims of medical identity theft.[39] This number is increasing as nowadays medical records are mostly stored electronically, which makes it easier for hackers to collect them.

The terrifying thing is that a criminal can come into possession not only of data which can help them to make financial gains but the consequences of that type of crime may be fatal. Let us assume that the perpetrator of the crime tinkers with the patient's medical record data, for example with the information about allergies or blood type. Then, in the event of the need of a quick medical help for the unconscious patient, a doctor quickly reviews such information and administers drugs which in reality are not to be administered. Because of identity theft, the patient is now fighting for their life. What is more, medical records can be stolen to obtain the patient's personal information with a view to selling

---

36 http://www.law.umich.edu/special/exoneration/Pages/casedetail.aspx?caseid=3061, last access: April 9, 2018.
37 http://krebsonsecurity.com/2015/05/carefirst-blue-cross-breach-hits-1-1m/, last access: April 9, 2018.
38 http://www.forbes.com/sites/laurashin/2015/05/29/why-medical-identity-theft-is-rising-and-how-to-protect-yourself/#62e36159e200, last access: April 9, 2018.
39 R. Douglas, *Identity Theft and Scan Prevention Services*: http://www.identitytheft.info/medical.aspx, last access: April 9, 2018.

it on the black market. As already stated, a Social Security Number as well as stolen medical identities can be bought through underground websites for $50. Other potential consequences resulting from stealing someone's medical record include false medical bills, false insurance claims, denial of employment caused by a false medical history, and, undoubtedly, time lost and expenses incurred in the process of rectifying the altered or false information.[40]

In recent years, medical data have been a prime target for cybercriminals. Regarding the statistics provided by the Identity Theft Resource Center, in 2014, 322 of the 761 data breaches fell into the medical category.[41] There is no doubt that medical identity theft destroys lives, damages credit ratings, and has dramatic consequences for someone's health. Medical identity theft, therefore, is one of the most dangerous types of identity theft as it may not only cause financial consequences but also become life-threatening.

3 Protection and prevention

Even though the scale of identity theft increases every year, there are steps which one can take so as not to become a victim. First of all, people should be aware of the existence of this phenomenon and of ways in which their identity can be stolen because without special knowledge it is impossible to battle the problem. Identity thieves collect personal data in many ways: by "dumpster diving," by stealing mail or hacking a computer, as well as by collecting them from reports or records. Typically, easy access to sensitive information is a result of unwise actions of an individual. People should realize that their personal data, which are of great value, must be used with reasonable diligence and should see to it that no unauthorized person use them. Any documents or papers in which any information about oneself can be found should be shred before consigning them to a trash bin. Setting the lock and a strong password which meets complexity requirement for the personal computer, email account, and websites where we use personal data can also save us from being an identity theft victim, as can protecting the PIN codes to debit or credit cards. What is more, telephone calls or questionnaires requesting personal information should never be responded to. All these steps should become part of a daily routine as they can prevent an identity theft attack and severe consequences which were mentioned above.

---

40 See the information from the U.S. Department of Health and Human Services: https://oig.hhs.gov/fraud/medical-id-theft/index.asp, last access: April 9, 2018.
41 S. D'Alfonso, *The Growing Problem of Medical Identity Theft*: https://securityintelligence.com/the-growing-problem-of-medical-identity-theft/, last access: April 9, 2018.

As a Social Security Number is said to be the most attractive and valuable piece of information to an identity thief,[42] it should be also well and carefully protected. Financial accounts and records as well as medical records (with particular attention to insurance claims) must be monitored regularly. It is also very important to monitor the children's credit reports regularly as it can take years until it is discovered that child identity theft has been committed. To facilitate the process, the website www.AnnualCreditReport.com has been created, where a free credit report can be obtained.

It is also a good idea to place a fraud alert or a security freeze on the credit record, which, depending on the state, can be done for free or for extra payment. However, even this small charge is worth paying to prevent the enormous financial consequences which may occur when someone uses someone else's identity for financial advantages. Placing the freezes allows for taking control over any transaction connected with the credit card or the account, person who accesses the credit report and time when it happens because the credit file is blocked until a person gives permission to release the blockade.[43] What is really important is that one does not have to be an identity theft victim to place a security freeze on a credit file.[44] A fraud alert is also a very useful tool, which can make it harder to use someone else's identity to open accounts in his or her name. A fraud alert means that when someone applies for a loan, the business must verify their identity before granting it, for example by contacting that person.[45]

Given the number of the victims of this crime and the unawareness of the society, many businesses have been set up which offer products and services designed to protect consumers from identity theft. There are also a lot of non-profit agencies which specialize in education and assistance as well as a great number of services dedicated to people who want to learn how they can be protected from identity theft. Finally, as this crime hits a greater number of Americans by the year, insurance companies have started to offer identity theft insurance policies to potential victims.[46]

---

42 https://wallethub.com/edu/identity-theft/17120/, last access: August 2016.
43 https://krebsonsecurity.com/2015/06/how-i-learned-to-stop-worrying-and-embrace-the-security-freeze/, last access: April 9, 2018.
44 C. Tundra, *Being An Identity Theft Victim: What I Did After To Protect Myself From Identity Theft*.
45 See the information from the Federal Trade Commission: https://www.consumer.ftc.gov/articles/0275-place-fraud-alert, last access: April 9, 2018.
46 See: R. Douglas, *Identity Theft and Scan Prevention Services*: http://www.identitytheft.info/diyidentitytheftprotection.aspx, last access: April 9, 2018.

Also, choosing technical and organizational solutions may help with reducing the scale of the identity theft phenomenon.[47] For example, the *Fair and Accurate Credit Transactions Act 2003* adopted the Identity Theft Red Flags Rule, which requires financial institutions which operate a transaction account belonging to a consumer to assess the risk of identity theft and detect the warning signs of identity theft in their day-to-day operations to create the solution to prevent the theft of their consumers' data.[48] What is more, the shredding laws order the destruction of documents containing personal data. Such regulations are provided for by such federal acts as *Fair and Accurate Credit Transactions Act 2003*, *Health Insurance Portability and Accountability Act 1996*, *Economic Espionage Act 1996*, *Serbane-Oxley Act 2002*, as well as by state acts, for example in Californian Civil Code 1798.80-82.[49] California was also the first state which introduced the notification obligation, in 2002 (1798.82 Civil Code).[50] In 2009, such a solution served as a model for the American Congress in their passing of the *Data Accountability and Trust Act*, which enforced the notification obligation on the federal level.[51]

To sum up, a great increase in the number of victims of identity theft led to the drafting of *The Identity Theft and Assumption Deterrence Act*. Even though there is no method which can save Americans from thieves, the more information we have about the phenomenon, the more steps we can take to prevent it. In a written testimony submitted in 2000 to the U.S. Senate Committee Hearing on the Judiciary Subcommittee on Technology, Terrorism and Government Information, Michelle Brown, a victim of identity fraud, stated: "it was a scenario I had only previously known through unbelievable stories painted in Hollywood: someone becomes you, erases your life, and through their destructive behaviors, complicates your own existence to an extreme level where you no longer know how to just live day after day. Your life becomes the life consumed by unraveling the unthinkable acts that your perpetrator has done in your perceived skin."[52]

---

47 A. Lach, *Karnoprawna reakcja na zjawisko kradzieży tożsamości*, Warsaw 2015, p. 147.
48 *Ibidem*, p. 152.
49 *Ibidem*, p. 153.
50 *Ibidem*, p. 156.
51 *Ibidem*, p. 158.
52 *Written Testimony of Michelle Brown:* https://www.privacyrights.org/written-testimony-michelle-brown, last access: April 9, 2018.

Maciej Barczewski and Aleksandra Czubek

Wearable Technology: Selected Legal Challenges Related to Big Data Collection

1 Introductory remarks

This chapter seeks to address selected legal issues arising in relation to the growth of the *wearable technology* industry. By defining *wearables* in the first place, it examines what legal concerns are deriving from the nature of those objects. Moreover, it will describe the impact of technological advances on the law in the data protection area and the upcoming changes, including the implementation of the new Data Protection Regulation. Finally, it will focus on the incorporation of *wearable technology* in selected areas. The paper will include an analysis of how *wearables* can improve the standard of employees' protection in the workplace and patients' conditions in the healthcare industry. Those two areas will be discussed as the first ones to have incorporated *wearables* as everyday use devices and as those that are fully regulated by laws. Moreover, *wearables*, designed to measure humans' performance and efficiency, sometimes even to enhance it, are most likely to be successfully used in these two areas. Hence, it seems reasonable to examine these two fields as good examples of the practical use of those devices.

2 Wearable technology – an attempt of a definition

By the end of the 20th century, as described by an IT (information technology) scientist Mahadev Satyanarayanan,[1] *wearable technology* became an important wave of new industry expansion. Known as *wearable technology* or simply *wearables,* they are portable body-worn devices, which constantly collect data about their user or their surroundings. The aim of data collection is to provide the user or third parties (various entities) with information on the user's performance, regarding the user's environment and conditions, generated in the course of using the device.

In his research, M. Satyanarayanan predicted the invention of electronic glasses, designed to provide the user with information about observed animate

---

[1] M. Satyanarayanan is a pioneer in the field of portable computers development.

and inanimate elements of the environment. To exemplify: looking at another person, the user would be able to discover their first and second name, mood, or basic current needs.[2] Moreover, observing flora or fauna through the glasses would allow the user to recognize certain species' needs, such as level of starvation or need for watering. About ten years later, Google Glasses were unveiled and, together with other sorts of body-worn, data-collecting electronic devices, entered the market.

It is worth noting that *wearable technology* is actually part of a broader phenomenon, i.e., "wearable computing." This will be defined as a "study or practice of inventing, designing, building, or using miniature body-borne computational and sensory devices. Wearable computers may be worn under, over, or in clothing, or may also be themselves clothes."[3] The development of this field is an effect of the expansion of the *ubiquitous computing* concept, which can be described as an idea of omnipresent computing technology,[4] currently often named the "Internet of Things."

In an attempt to encapsulate numerous descriptive considerations in a short definition, *wearable technology* should be understood as a category of technologically advanced devices containing built-in, often Internet-enabled microchips, as well as radio frequency identification (RFID) sensors,[5] collecting data about their user, usually designed for application onto the users' body, often as a piece of clothing or an accessory. Such devices can be worn on top of regular clothing, can be a part of it (built-in), or become an independent accessory. Alternatively, Danielle Wilde describes smart clothing as "interactively responsive garments and interfaces."[6]

---

2 M. Satyanarayanan, *Persuasive Computing: Vision and Challenges*, IEEE Personal Communications, https://www.cs.cmu.edu/~aura/docdir/pcs01.pdf, August, 2001, last accessed 07.04.18, p. 1.

3 S. Mann, *The encyclopedia of human–computer interaction. 23 wearable computing*, https://www.interaction-design.org/literature/book/the-encyclopedia-of-human-computer-interaction-2nd-ed/wearable-computing, last accessed 07.04.18.

4 A. Thierer, *The Internet of Things and Wearable Technology: Addressing Privacy and Security Concerns without Derailing Innovation*, Richmond Journal of Law & Technology, XXI(2), p. 2.

5 M. Cunningham, *Next Generation Privacy: The Internet of Things, Data Exhaust, and Reforming Regulation by Risk of Harm*, Groningen Journal of International Law, 2014, 2(2), p. 115.

6 *The future of wearable technologies, conversation EDU*, https://www.youtube.com/watch?v=i3CKsuv0Sbk, last accessed 07.04.18.

In the process of defining *wearable technology*, it is necessary to indicate what characteristic mandatory features a device has to display to be included in the *wearables* category. However, it needs to be noted that such features do not have to exist cumulatively for a device to be considered as *wearable technology*.[7] For instance, the necessity for a device to be constantly attached to human (user's) body is a feature of many of wearable devices (i.e., Google Glass, smart glasses, or clothing made of fabric equipped with special measurement sensors) and those satisfy the condition of constant attachment to the user's body. On the other hand, Ralph Lauren's *Ricky Bag with Light*[8] (a bag equipped with a LED light and a power bank), which is also classified as *wearable technology*, does not require constant contact with the surface of the user's body to be able to work properly and fully realize its purposes.

Among the features which a *wearable technology* device should display, some are worth special emphasis and description:

- as the term implies, such a device should be a body-worn appliance, to allow for constant contact between human body and a device (or sensors together with certain parameter readers that are part of it);[9]
- an important feature of wearables is that they are connected to the Internet – networked,[10] designed to be able, through this feature, to collect, process, and analyze data about the user;
- as a group of personal devices, unlike many up-to-date technological devices, (i.e., tablets, cameras), *wearables* are meant to belong to one particular user and are designed to collect personal data about that person, and do not include features that allow for sharing them;[11]
- those devices are not fixed to a particular location and are simply connected to their user, not to a place they are or might be located at. For instance, some *wearables* are designed for surveillance purposes and they are likely to change the approach toward the means of surveillance.[12]
- once turned on, *wearable technology* devices are constantly in the "standby" mode. They are not designed to be turned on and off at the user's discretion.

---

7   R. Mathys, *Legal challenges of wearable computing*, Basel 2014, p. 6.
8   http://www.ralphlauren.com/product/index.jsp?productId=51156936, last accessed 07.04.18.
9   A.Thierer, *The Internet of things…*, p. 25.
10 *Ibidem*, p. 2.
11 Roland Mathys, *Legal…*, p. 6.
12 *Ibidem*, p. 6.

Because of the measurement purposes, those devices are designed to work constantly, at least in the "ready to operate" mode.[13]
- devices of that category are designed to be very sensitive to any environment factors, so that they can collect information regarding any parameters of the user, such as location, weather conditions, user's biomedical data, etc. and are capable of storing these data in designated Internet locations, such as "clouds;"
- one of the most important expectations toward *wearable technology* is that it should not limit its user's mobility. This is why such garment pieces are required to be designed in such a way as to fit the user and not limit their performance during regular everyday activities, or even enhance it, during e.g., sports performance;[14]
- finally, an extremely important feature these days is that those devices have to be not only functional apparel pieces but also objects of consumers' desires. They have to satisfy the sense of esthetics and remain an element of users' closets, as similar as possible to basic ones, not packed with technological value.[15]

The aforementioned features are the crucial characteristics of *wearables*. However, it needs to be stressed that the list is not exhaustive. Moreover, an object does not have to display all those cumulatively to be considered part of *wearable technology*. Furthermore, as it is a constantly developing field of technology, definitions are still flexible and subject to change or relevant adjustment. This is why the above list of characteristics is an open catalog. Nonetheless, those features distinguish wearables from other sorts of electronic devices.

3 Wearable technology as a Big Data collection source

The integration of modern technologies and the fashion industry can, and often does, lead to the creation of intelligent apparel, defined as *wearable technology*. The miniaturization of any electronic equipment and the reduction of the costs of technologies enabling users to collect Big Data inevitably lead to the inclusion of those systems in the clothing environment and, broadly speaking, fashion

---

13   *Ibidem*.
14   S. Mann, J. Nolan, B. Wellman, *Sousveillance: Inventing and Using Wearable Computing Devices for Data Collection in Surveillance Environments*, Surveillance & Society 1(3), pp. 331–355, 337.
15   R. Mathys, "*Legal challenges…*", pp. 5–7.

industry. Wireless technologies are evolving, and fashion industry is not lagging behind, adapting technological solutions to its products.

As any development, the growth of the wearable technology market brings both advantages and legal challenges deriving from the expansion of the branch. All processes of creation, production, sales, and finally exploiting newly developed goods will have to comply with newly set or adapted legal rules. It needs to be noted that body-borne technologies will raise a number of safety and privacy concerns and one of the crucial legal challenges, which is emerging due to the wearable technology industry development, is the case of data collection. The right to data collection, processing, and analysis, together with their safe storage, is the key issue, and a challenge to the designers, producers, and retailers, who will be responsible for the wearable technology distribution.[16] It has to be mentioned that according to most legal definitions in the European legal framework the majority of data collected by wearable devices are considered as personal and are subject to legal protection under the data privacy regime, not only as personal data but often also as what is known as sensitive data. Currently, the regulation of such data can be found in Article 8 of the Data Protection Directive, which governs a number of legal issues arising in the context of data-collecting items.[17]

Wearable technology is essentially data-gathering devices, providing information related to their users[18] and designed to constantly analyze its users' characteristics. The aim of this process is not only to provide the user with information about their performance and activity but also, very often, to pass this information to a recipient who is an entity separate from the user. Among those recipients, we can find a number of different entities, such as device producer/provider, a doctor who examines their patient (who at the same time is the user of a wearable device), an employer who provides their staff members with wearable devices, or any other subject who could potentially benefit from gathering and analyzing users' personal data.[19]

---

16 A. Thierer, *The Internet of Things and Wearable Technology: Addressing Privacy and Security Concerns without Derailing Innovation*, Richmond Journal of Law & Technology, XXI(2), p. 2.
17 Guidelines on the Rights of Individuals with regard to the Processing of Personal Data: https://secure.edps.europa.eu/EDPSWEB/webdav/site/mySite/shared/Documents/Supervision/Guidelines/14-02-25_GL_DS_rights_EN.pdf; (2014), last accessed 07.04.2018, p. 7.
18 R. Mathys, *Legal challenges of wearable computing*, Basel 2014, p. 13.
19 A. Thierer, *The Internet*..., p. 33.

As a consequence, legal challenges arising in light of the development of wearable technology should be considered from two perspectives: firstly, in the context of the process of devices' production, products' preparation for market introduction, their inclusion in consumer trading, and their functioning in the legal framework generally; secondly, at the stage of products' usage and operation. At this stage, any resulting ambiguities will be taken to courts and a general jurisdiction will have to be established, based on the existing legal structure, which is not following technology in terms of its modernity.[20]

To avoid the discussion on the subject of the connection between *wearable tech* and Big Data on an abstract level, it is essential to provide several examples of devices introduced in the market offer of clothing manufacturers. Such enterprises base their products' assets on a combination of data-collecting technology and appealing design, creating demand among consumers.

Firstly, fashion house Ralph Lauren, after a great success of its first product combining fashion and technology, i.e., *Ricky Bag with Light*, a traditionally designed bag equipped with a LED light and a portable battery allowing to charge a smartphone, took a step further with their line of *PoloTech* sport t-shirts.[21] These t-shirts are worn for the purpose of tracking the user's workout and collecting such data as the user's pulse, heartbeat, etc. Special fibers included in the t-shirt's fabric collect and transmit information via Bluetooth to the user's smartphone. A similar device was produced by the Under Armour Inc. company, which introduced an innovative means of workout tracking, located in chest-based belts, examining the user's data during their workout.[22] A completely different "device" was released by a French designer *Spinali Designs* under the name of *Connected Swimsuit Creations*, a bikini sunbathing suit whose purpose is to protect its users from sunburn and a harmful influence of ultraviolet rays on their skin. The bikini has special sensors which measure the number of rays which reach the user's body during sunbathing and sends a message to the user's smartphone when, according to the data collected, it is necessary to use a sunscreen again, in order to avoid sunburn or unhealthy tan.[23]

---

20 L. Berglin, *Smart Textiles and Wearable Technology A Report within the Baltic Fashion Project*, 2013, Swedish School of Textiles, pp. 9–11, available at: https://www.diva-portal.org/smash/get/diva2:884011/FULLTEXT01.pdf, last accessed 07.04.2018.
21 The Polotech Shirt, Ralph Lauren: http://www.ralphlauren.com/product/index.jsp?productId=69917696, last accessed 05.04.2016.
22 Fitness Devices, Under Armour: https://www.underarmour.com/en-ca/armour39-module-and-strap/pid1255371, last accessed 07.04.2018.
23 Smart Connected Bikini; Spinali Design: http://www.spinali-design.com/collections/neviano-intelligent-swimsuit-women, last accessed 07.04.2018.

After considering these examples, it needs to be emphasized that the relationship between Big Data and *wearable technology* is not only of a functional nature. The growth of *wearable technology* industry affects the legislation by creating a broad scope of legal matters which are called "the new generation of legal challenges" to both legal theoreticians and practitioners but also, and mainly, to the legislator on both national and international level.[24] Issues arising around wearable devices will be mainly related to privacy and data safety, but also to the ownership of data, questioning who has the right to them and whose property are they.[25]

Data collected by intelligent pieces of garment are information which can be related to health, user's wellness and comfort, biomedical information, skin parameters, any substances released by the body during physical activity, or subjects' geolocation, all inevitably related to a particular entity: a natural person.[26] All these items of information are collected, gathered, and analyzed in the course of the user's daily activity as he or she is using the device, which at the same time keeps track of their actions. This brings the issue of access to collected information and its management. Preferably, from the data protection perspective, it should be a user's feature to have access to collected and analyzed data. However, this would prevent the producer of the device from obtaining important information. Moreover, regulations restricting access to collected data to the device user would, for instance due to professional secrecy, prevent the usage of *wearables* in many areas, such as workplace or medical analytics, for which those devices were designed in the first place.[27]

On the other hand, if the producer was given unlimited access to data gathered by smart devices, a legislation complying with the existing and upcoming privacy framework would have to be reinvented and would never receive positive evaluation. In sum, the more accessible the personal data gathered by intelligent garments are, the less likely it is that the data privacy objectives will be met.

A question of access to the collected data automatically raises another one, i.e., that of the ownership of collected information. Furthermore, after establishing who is in possession of a valuable dataset gathered by intelligent

---

24 A. Bevitt, H. Swan, *Challenges with the Workplace Wearables in the EU and US*, Privacy & Data Protection, p. 1.
25 I. Rubinstein, *Big Data: The End of Privacy or the New Beginning?*, International Data Privacy Law, January 25, 2013, p. 1.
26 R. Mathys, *Legal...*, pp. 5–7.
27 J. Steenhuysen, *Beyond Fitbit: The Quest to Develop Medical-grade Wearables*, Westlaw Journal Medical Devices, January 12, 2016, WESTLAW™ International, p. 2.

pieces of garment, a question about analytics and merchandizing of such information arises. There is a whole range of opportunities that selling that kind of goods would create, if it were legally possible to, e.g., sell collected biomedical information to medical services. As a consequence, those services would be able to offer methods of treatment well suited to any particular entity, without extra effort or time spent on analyzing their condition in medical units. At this point, it needs to be mentioned that selling such information is problematic, mainly because it is related to ultimately personal and intimate data, which, according to the existing legal framework and ethical standards, is impossible without a previous consent of the data subject.

That rule was first mentioned in Recital 30 of the Data Protection Directive[28], hereinafter DPD, and will continue to exist in the upcoming data protection legislation, i.e., the General Data Protection Regulation (GDPR), which comes into force in May 2018.[29] The Data Subjects consent itself, which is a matter of high importance in the context of *wearables,* is also explicitly defined in Article 2 (h) of the DPD Data Protection Directive.

Moreover, what might be a matter of legal discussion in relation to the *wearable tech* concept is the question of when the breach of privacy would become not only the issue between two parties such as the producer of goods and the user but also affect a separate third party existing in the user's vicinity.[30] An example of such privacy infringement is using *Google Glass* in public. This kind of a device augments the user's perception of the reality, allowing them to access the data downloaded by the glasses form the Internet.[31] When it concerns inanimate elements of the environment, it can be considered the user's support, helping them to recognize the features of the surroundings (i.e., when used by visually impaired people as a means of navigation) and therefore to get around in a more convenient, easier way.[32] However, such devices also provide information about animate elements of the environment, i.e., other people, whose privacy is normally protected by law. The data collected are obviously varied, depending

---

28 Directive 95/46/EC of the European Parliament and of the Council of October 24, 1995 on the protection of individuals with regard to the processing of personal data and on the free movement of such data [1995] OJ 2 281/31-50, hereinafter: DPD.
29 General Data Protection Regulation [2016] OJ 2 119/1-88, hereinafter: GDPR.
30 A. Thierer, *The Internet…*, p. 67.
31 Z. Corbyn, *Google Glass – Wearable Tech but Would You Wear It?*, The Guardian, April 6, 2014; https://www.theguardian.com/technology/2014/apr/06/google-glass-technology-smart-eyewear-camera-privacy, last accessed 07.04.2018.
32 A. Thierer, *The Internet…*, p. 22.

on the device, but to use *Google Glass* as an example, by looking through them at another person, the user can obtain such items of information as the object's name, surname, or current mood, all of them then delivered to the *Google Glass* user and in some cases also to the device provider.[33]

4 Legal regulations concerning collection, analysis and Big Data processing by *wearable technology* devices in the EU and the United States

The primary difference between the respective legal frameworks of the European Union (EU) and the United States (US) regarding the protection of personal data collected by electronic devices is that in the EU countries there is a harmonized legislation, whereas in the US there is no unitary legal act which would collectively state legal order in this area. Thus, such laws can be found in various legal acts which relate to other areas of law.

On 24 October 1995, Directive (EC) 95/46 of the European Parliament and of the Council on the protection of individuals with regard to the processing of personal data and on the free movement of such data (hereinafter DPD) was amended.[34] The Directive is at the moment considered the most influential privacy law[35] as it has become a unitary regulation for the issues of collection and personal data processing, including biomedical data gathered by *wearable technology* devices. Currently, the new GDPR has been passed by the European Parliament and will be coming into force in May 2018. Significantly, its rules are going to apply to any businesses, organizations, or entities targeting EU consumers, regardless of their geographic location.[36]

The current DPD establishes some core rules for the privacy of personal data which are to be understood as "any information relating to an identified or identifiable natural person ('data subject'); an identifiable person is one who can be identified, directly or indirectly, in particular by reference to an identification number or to one or more factors specific to his physical, physiological, mental,

---

33 *Ibidem*, p. 112.
34 European Parliament and Council Directive 95/46/EC of 24 October 1995 on the protection of individuals with regard to the processing of personal data and on the free movement of such data [Official Journal L 281 of 23.11.1995].
35 I. Rubinstein, *Big Data...*, p. 1.
36 'EU Approves GDPR' [2016] 50(4) Information Management Journal, p. 7.

economic, cultural or social identity."[37] The rationale of establishing those rules was to allow only for legally approved processing of those data. Article 6 of the Directive states the standard of data processing, which requires data to be processed fairly and lawfully, collected for specified, explicit, and legitimate purposes and not further processed in a way incompatible with those purposes. Moreover, it states that further processing of data shall be "adequate, relevant, and not excessive in relation to the purposes for which they are collected and/or further processed." In compliance with DPD provisions, data collected have to be accurate and updated if necessary. Data which are "inaccurate or incomplete, having regard to the purposes for which they were collected or for which they are further processed, shall be erased or rectified."[38] Regarding data maintenance, data shall be kept in a form which permits identification of data subjects for no longer than is necessary for the purposes for which the data were collected or for which they are further processed.

Furthermore, Articles 2 h and 7 a stipulate that the permission for data processing needs to be obtained. The following articles (10[39] and 11[40]) specify the obligation of transparency for entities that have access to collected data and hence data identification, confidentiality and safety. These are the basic standards, regulated by the European framework, which any objects (devices) that are designed to collect data should comply with. That also applies to *wearable technology*, which collects Big Data generated by its user operating any kind of a device.

Let us apply the abovementioned to an example that would take a theoretical debate to a practical level: a "smartwatch," for instance, has to comply with the standards set out in the DPD to be introduced into trade in Europe. The device's terms and conditions of use have to be in compliance with the established rules and additionally, a set of rules should be in place regarding how to standardize

---

37 Article 2 (a); European Parliament and Council Directive 95/46/EC of 24 October 1995 on the protection of individuals with regard to the processing of personal data and on the free movement of such data [Official Journal L 281 of 23.11.1995].
38 Article 6 European Parliament and Council Directive 95/46/EC of 24 October 1995 on the protection of individuals with regard to the processing of personal data and on the free movement of such data [Official Journal L 281 of 23.11.1995].
39 Article 10 European Parliament and Council Directive 95/46/EC of 24 October 1995 on the protection of individuals with regard to the processing of personal data and on the free movement of such data [Official Journal L 281 of 23.11.1995].
40 Article 11 European Parliament and Council Directive 95/46/EC of 24 October 1995 on the protection of individuals with regard to the processing of personal data and on the free movement of such data [Official Journal L 281 of 23.11.1995].

similar devices that will be appearing in the market, as well as the mode of receiving and processing users' consent to their personal data usage by the designer/seller/producer.

Aside from these principles, the DPD also seeks to provide free and legal personal data movement to states which are not the EU Member States. Moreover, it seeks to harmonize foreign jurisdictions and administrative rules.[41] In the context of the *wearable technology* issues, it is crucial to achieve the harmonized judicial and legal consensus, as the market in this field is growing globally, not only within the EU. Due to the multipurpose activity (the combination of such fields as science, art, or medicine) during the production and distribution of *wearable technology* goods, it is crucial to moderate the laws in such a way that the object could function in the international commerce.

As mentioned before, the Directive cannot be considered a legal structure that is in keeping with the technological advances and as a regulation is not sufficient anymore, given the demands of the data-collecting devices market. Accordingly, in the past few years, the European Commission has commenced works on the modernization of regulations. According to the published Communication, the Directive could no longer meet the challenges of "rapid technological developments and globalisation."[42] The Commission's initial idea of the changes emphasized standard data protection measures such as imposing stricter rules governing the process of giving consent, strengthening transparency, and clarifying and making more explicit certain preconditions of data protection, including data minimization and the right of access.[43] As a result of the presented concerns, the Commission introduced the GDPR.[44] The contents of the Regulation clearly show that the Commission was well aware of the

---

41 Recital 56 of the European Parliament and Council Directive 95/46/EC of 24 October 1995 on the protection of individuals with regard to the processing of personal data and on the free movement of such data [Official Journal L 281 of 23.11.1995].
42 European Commission Communication, "*A comprehensive approach on personal data protection in the European Union*", COM (2010) 609 final.
43 I. Rubinstein, *Big Data…*, p. 2.
44 Impact Assessment (including annexes) accompanying the proposed Regulation (Regulation of the European Parliament and of the Council on the protection of individuals with regard to the processing of personal data and on the free movement of such data, GDPR) and the proposed Directive (Directive of the European Parliament and of the Council on the protection of individuals with regard to the processing of personal data by competent authorities for the purposes of prevention, investigation, detection or prosecution of criminal offences or the execution of criminal penalties, and the free movement of such data), SEC (2012) 72 final.

"dramatic technological changes" that had occurred since the DPD was first proposed and very concerned with problems raised by profiling and data mining.[45] For instance, the Regulation introduces several new privacy rights, such as the right to be forgotten and to data portability.[46]

On the other hand, in the US, there is no unitary legal regulation which would constitute data privacy protection over information processed by data-collecting *wearable technology*. Moreover, there is no core regulation which can be considered a point of reference for the producers and users of Big Data-generating devices. Existing within the US legal framework, both users and entrepreneurs introducing *wearable tech* to the market often seem to be unaware of what rules they should comply with when using or producing the devices. This is because there exist few or no points of reference with that respect, despite courts' rulings and judicature.[47] There used to be an idea to apply *Consumer Privacy Bill of Rights Act*, but it never translated into any actual legislation.[48] Most of the current legislation in the US referring to the issue of *wearable technology* is at the moment regulated by various separate laws, a patchwork of state laws, and sector and industry specific federal and state laws and regulations, which mainly apply to certain circumstances in which such devices might be used. That said, different acts apply when a device is being used in the workplace or for the purposes of healthcare.[49] For instance, as regards the use of health-related wearables, such as pedometers and other activity trackers, in addition to corporate wellness programs, the provisions of both the *Health Insurance Portability and Accountability Act*[50] (HIPAA) and the *Americans with Disabilities Act*[51] (the ADA) are applicable.

---

45 *Ibidem*, pp. 24–25.
46 I. Rubinstein, *Big Data…*, p. 2.
47 A. Bevitt, H. Swan, *Challenges…*, p. 2.
48 A. Chernichaw, B. Freeman, *White & Case Technology Newsflash*, April 08, 2015: http://www.whitecase.com/publications/article/white-house-re-introduces-consumer-privacy-bill-rights-act, last accessed 07.04.2018.
49 A. Bevitt, H. Swan, *Challenges…*, p. 2.
50 Health Insurance Portability and Accountability Act of 1996; Public Law 104 - 191, 104th Congress: https://www.gpo.gov/fdsys/pkg/PLAW-104publ191/html/PLAW-104publ191.htm, last accessed 07.04.2018.
51 Americans with Disabilities Act of 1990 - 42 U.S. Code Chapter 126: https://www.ada.gov/pubs/adastatute08.htm, last accessed 07.08.2018.

5 Wearable technology in the workplace

5.1 The risks and advantages of incorporating *wearable technology* into the work environment

The development of technological solutions is in many cases supposed to lead to the enhancement of human capabilities, a person's efficiency and productivity in all areas of life. Consequently, any technological innovations are immediately transferred to, or are very often designed from the very beginning to be used in, the professional environment, i.e., in the workplace of various types. This pattern also applies to *wearable technology*. The advantages of introducing such devices in the workplace are mostly based on the fact that they are designed to control the employees' productivity, enhance their wellness and well-being, or communicate possible ways of achieving it. What is more, such devices have certain features which help protect the employees from strains and health damage, raise their efficiency and effectiveness, and see increased levels of abiding by health and safety rules in the work environment. All the aforementioned features and ways of their measurement are obviously related to the type of device being used in any particular case.[52]

Undoubtedly, all of the aforementioned results of introducing *wearable tech* at work would positively influence not only the employer's perspective but also the employees' situation. Nevertheless, the need to regulate the usage of data-collecting devices as a part of a workplace policy is inevitable. Legal challenges related to this subject bring up the question of whether the difficulties associated with the required legal structure and its novel nature do not outweigh the positive factors.[53]

According to a survey conducted by PricewaterhouseCoopers, 70% of employees would agree to wear and use *wearable technology* devices provided by their employer, and as a consequence assent to their personal data being collected for the analytics purpose in exchange for a reduction on their insurance premiums.[54] These results show the idea of integrating the profits of both environments, employers' and employees' alike, which would derive from the introduction of *wearables* to the workplace. The profits mean, on one hand, data

---

[52] S. Mann, J. Nolan, B. Wellman, *Sousveillance...*, p. 342.
[53] N. Sansom, *Wearable Technology in the Workplace*, Cyberspace Lawyer, March 2015, WESTLAW™ International, p. 1.
[54] Consumer Intelligence Series, *The Future of Wearables*, PricewaterhouseCoopers LLP: http://www.pwc.com/us/en/technology/publications/wearable-technology.html, last accessed 07.08.2018.

collection and the possibility of using the data analytics outcome to increase the productivity and efficiency or safety of employees, at the same time decreasing some of the contributions related e.g., to the work insurance policy and leading to an increased direct income level.[55]

As already mentioned, one of the main challenges related to the introduction of *wearables* to the work environment is the fact that those devices are designed mainly to allow the employers to collect and process their employees' personal data. Clearly, the purpose of gathering these data is mostly meant to lead to bilateral benefits, such as increasing the workers' efficiency or safety in the work space, along with introducing many profitable programs that employees can participate in, although the necessity to regulate this area of processing personal data by the employer is pressing.

Primarily, within the respective jurisdictions of the US and the EU, whenever the employer considers the implementation of wearables in the work space, they ought to make sure that the stage of compliance with the transparency rule is sufficient. The type of data collected, their amount, method of processing, or destinations to which they are being processed have to remain transparent. Reinforcing the transparency of processing and providing a meaningful notice of data practices and actual choice to opt out of unwanted collection, use, or disclosure of personal data are the most reasonable ways to comply with the existing laws for personal data processing.[56] What is more, after receiving the employees' consent to process their personal data, it needs to be outlined what kind of entities are going to have access to the data collected.

In the course of introducing data-collecting devices to the work environment, or including in the existing team a new staff member who is using *wearable technology* at work, it is necessary to obtain the employees' consent for the use of such devices. Moreover, they need to express their consent to operating in the space/environment where such devices are being used by others, as that may influence third parties as well. Some devices have such a broad scope of operation that they have an impact on the user's entire surroundings, for instance by analyzing the immediate environment. For that reason, consent has to be acquired both for the personal use of the device by an employee as well as for remaining in the ambience of constant data collection

---

55 R. Mathys, *Legal...*, p. 16.
56 N. Richards, J. King, *Big Data and the future for privacy*, October 19, 2014; Handbook of Research on Digital Transformations Elgar 2016, pp. 17–18.

Regarding the necessity to obtain the employees' consent, a policy has to be legally regulated toward those who disagree to using *wearables* or operating in the space equipped with them. This is a risky issue, as it can easily lead to discrimination accusations. What is more, it needs to be stated at which stage the refusal can be communicated and whether that can result in the employee's transfer or dismissal from the position held or not hiring them for the position offered.[57]

Another issue that might be brought up while *wearable technology* is announced in the form of devices designed to measure parameters of the work setting is the danger of creating unnatural, hermetic groups of colleagues, distinguished from each other by means of sharing some characteristic features measured by *wearable tech*. Wristband fitness trackers can serve as an example. Most of them, while tracking daily activities (steps, stairs climbed, calories burnt etc.) automatically publish the results online, comparing them to others. Additionally, they often share these data with third parties, i.e., stakeholders who show interest in receiving such information. That is why in enterprises that offer *wearable technology* as a kind of gratuity employees should be able to refuse to use them. By generating rivalry, measured by fitness trackers among staff members, it is extremely easy to generate results different from those anticipated: instead of integrating staff members, *wearable technology* can easily lead to alienating those members who decide not to participate. Consequently, instead of building a strong structure in the workplace, repercussions can be destructive and discriminatory. These concerns are becoming a serious legal challenge as all of them can be grounds for court litigations.[58]

In the context of the issue of discrimination, the meaning of "adequate data management" should be also examined. According to the respective jurisdictions of the EU and the US, one of the most important factors in protecting data collected by *wearable technology* used at work is creating such a method of data processing and analysis that would deny access to the results to people involved in the decision-making process in the companies' structure. As explained above, horizontal discrimination in the workplace can be a consequence of using *wearables* at work. On the other hand, vertical discrimination could be also based on the information collected by devices. Again, to exemplify, fitness activity measured by *wearables* and scores achieved could influence promotion

---

57 B. Dzida, K. Healy, D. Mendel, *Wearable technology and global employment rights – what employers need to know*, Freshfields Bruckhaus, Deringer, September 9, 2015: http://knowledge.freshfields.com/en/global/r/1485/wearable_technology_and_global_employment_rights_-_what, last accessed 07.08.2018.
58 A. Bevitt, H. Swan, *Challenges with workplace…*, pp. 2–3.

decisions only because a person responsible for such arrangements has decided to reward people who are involved in intense physical activity.[59] That would lead to unfair treatment of those who have different priorities, or who decide not to share their personal data collected.

Another risk that could possibly follow the introduction of *wearable technology* as a part of a "work uniform" is the danger of using advanced technology for collecting data considered as corporate valuable information. It needs to be noted that such devices are often capable of registering data, information, conversations, or taking pictures, which can lead to unregistered leaks of information, all that because the employer provides their staff with such devices as part of their everyday uniforms. Difficulties in monitoring and controlling collected information can become a serious issue as a malpractice detrimental to the employer and the company itself.[60]

To conclude this section, it is worth posing a question of where the boundaries between "protecting privacy" and creating or keeping secrets are. Some data, even personal, although related to the employees' biomedical parameters, are at the same time information which the employer receives about their staff members anyway. The way of collecting it is different than using *wearable technology* devices and its options but still has similar effects. Let us consider measuring employees' work efficiency: through *wearables,* energy levels can be easily and precisely monitored. Thus, the device can reveal whether a person is fully engaged in fulfilling his or hers duties.

5.2 Legal regulations regarding Data Privacy in the EU and the US and *wearable technology* in the work environment

The EU Member States laws provide that data collected by the smart clothing arranged for by the employer are subject to legal protection under "the general conditions governing the lawfulness of data processing" included in the EC 95/46 Directive.[61] However, in terms of further legal acts, when implementing the Directive to the national legal systems, some employers may still be bound by stricter legal requirements when providing their employees with technologically equipped, activity-tracking pieces of uniforms. An example can be presented

---

59 A. Thierer, *The Internet of things…*, pp. 98–99.
60 A. Bevitt, H. Swan, *Challenges with workplace…*, p. 4.
61 European Parliament and Council Directive 95/46/EC of 24 October 1995 on the protection of individuals with regard to the processing of personal data and on the free movement of such data [Official Journal L 281 of 23.11.1995].

based on the German system, where introducing new means of monitoring the employees should be preceded by consultations with the work council.[62]

Due to the diversity in the scope of implementing the Directive and with the incredible pace of technological development and an increased necessity for more precise legal solutions, the European Commission, in January 2012, presented a draft regulation of the European system of personal data protection, which was supposed to be standardized in compliance with the demands of technological development.[63] As a consequence of that and other actions, as mentioned before, in May 2018, a unified European Regulation known as the GDPR will come into force.

Nevertheless, the draft regulation, in the phase of construction, provided some clarification on issues the existing Directive does not clarify. What is more, it offers the harmonization of provisions in order not to create differences between the legal systems across the member states with regard to personal data protection. Eventually, the projects resulted in the introduction of the Regulation of the European Parliament and of the Council of 27 April 2016 on the protection of natural persons with regard to the processing of personal data and on the free movement of such data, and repealing Directive 95/46/EC.[64]

Importantly, according to Article 288 of the Treaty on the Functioning of the European Union (TFEU),[65] as in force today, the European directives, in terms of their implementation, are subject to the "national authorities" of the Member States decisions, who are responsible for choosing "forms and methods" of the directives' application to the national law systems. Unlike the European directives, the GDPR does not require any provisions enacting the legislation to be passed by the national governments.[66] As a legislation, it intends to strengthen and unify data protection for individuals within the EU. It addresses the export of personal data outside the EU, navigating toward better international integration in the scope of data processing.[67] In a nutshell, the main objective of the GDPR

---

62 A. Bevitt, H. Swann, *Challenges with workplace…*, p. 2.
63 *Ibidem*, p. 4.
64 Regulation 2016/679 of the European Parliament and of the Council of 27 April 2016 on the protection of natural persons with regard to the processing of personal data and on the free movement of such data, and repealing Directive 95/46/EC (GDPR).
65 Article 288 of the Treaty on the Functioning of the European Union [2007] OJ 1 326/47.
66 S. Blackmer (May 5, 2016), *GDPR: Getting Ready for the New EU General Data Protection Regulation*, Information Law Group, InfoLawGroup LLP.
67 M. Stephens, *General Data Protection Regulation. Governance Risk and Assurance*: http://www.moorestephens.co.uk/MediaLibsAndFiles/media/MooreStephensUK/

is the reinforcement of individuals' rights, while supporting endless free flows of personal data in the digital market.[68] Heavy emphasis is placed on increasing the trust in the use of information society services (which include *wearables*) by EU users, both individuals and legal persons providing the services, while protecting their fundamental rights (in this context mainly privacy rights).[69] It is also important to notice that the GDPR would apply also to data controllers not established in the EU but capable of and actively processing EU residents' personal data (Article 3(2) of the GDPR). In the context of *wearables* and Big Data processing, that provision is an extremely important factor in the transborder data flow. Given that, first of all, many information society services conducted by the IoT (Internet of Things) devices, and, in general, any data-related activity conducted by those devices can be operated from all corners of the world, and that the IoT stakeholders can be based almost anywhere, it is important to realize that even in such cases the processed personal data should be protected (even if the specific means of data collection complies with all other data protection requirements).

The Regulation specifies some important matters, especially regarding the subject of *wearable technology* as personal data-collecting devices provided by the employer. First of all, it states far stricter methods of obtaining the employee's consent to their personal data being collected and processed at work, using the provided devices. According to the Directive, Article 2 (h) "the data subject's consent' shall mean any freely given specific and informed indication of his wishes by which the data subject signifies his agreement to personal data relating to him being processed."[70] Meanwhile, according to the Regulation, Article 4 (11), "'consent' of the data subject means any freely given, specific, informed and <u>unambiguous indication of the data</u> subject's wishes by which he or she, <u>by a statement</u>

Documents/GRA-The-EU_General-Data-Protection-Regulation.pdf?ext=.pdf, last accessed 07.04.2018.
68 F. Turton, *Shifting the Burden of Consent under the GDPR* (SCL The IT Law Community): https://www.scl.org/articles/3598-shifting-the-burden-of-consent-under-the-gdpr, last accessed May 26, 2017.
69 European Commission, Commission Communication to the European Parliament, the Council, the Economic and Social Committee and the Committee of the Regions. A coherent framework for building trust in the Digital Single Market for e-commerce and online services. 11 January 2012.
70 Article 2 (h) of the European Parliament and Council Directive 95/46/EC of 24 October 1995 on the protection of individuals with regard to the processing of personal data and on the free movement of such data [Official Journal L 281 of 23.11.1995].

or by a clear affirmative action, signifies agreement to the processing of personal data relating to him or her."[71] According to those changes, before receiving the consent, the employer will have to provide the employee with the specified and unambiguous information describing what kind of data, and by what means, are going to be collected. Also the method of stating their agreement will have to be completely clear.

In the US, the privacy of personal data is protected by a number of regulations different in individual states, in which they are amended and also enacted by the Federal Trade Commission, the Act of 1914, which, pursuant to Section 5 of the Act,[72] is entitled to undertake legislative actions aimed against unfair trade competition and unfair (misleading) actions or trade practice.[73]

As a consequence of the introduction of *wearable technology* in the workplace, some of the laws—both federal and state—protect employees. For instance, many states (i.e., Carolina, Connecticut, Florida, Hawaii) require obtaining the consent of all parties to recording conversations. This is the so-called "two party consent law," as opposed to "one party consent law." This rule is reflected in §632 California Penal Code.[74] It needs to be emphasized that in said law, the last section, (f), specifies that the rule does not apply to devices supporting hearing, used by handicapped persons, who are forced to use it due to their disability. ("This section does not apply to the use of hearing aids and similar devices, by persons afflicted with impaired hearing, for the purpose of overcoming the impairment to permit the hearing of sounds ordinarily audible to the human ear.")[75] In this respect, smart clothing which provides the recording function will increase the risk of violating these regulations.

---

71 Article 4 (11) of the Regulation 2016/679 of the European Parliament and of the Council of 27 April 2016 on the protection of natural persons with regard to the processing of personal data and on the free movement of such data, and repealing Directive 95/46/EC (GDPR).
72 Federal Trade Commission Act, Section 5: https://www.law.cornell.edu/uscode/text/15/45, last accessed 07.08.2018.
73 A. Mokrysz - Olszyńska; *Unfairness doctrine i podejście ekonomiczne do ochrony konsumentów w praktyce Federalnej Komisji Handlu w USA*; Ekonomia i Prawo, VII, 2011, p. 110.
74 California Penal Code, §632: http://www.leginfo.ca.gov/cgi-bin/displaycode?section=pen&group=00001-01000&file=630-638.53, last accessed 07.04.2018.
75 *Ibidem*, 632 (f).

Furthermore, in the U.S., the devices designed to measure health conditions in the work environment are subject to national regulations such as HIPAA[76] and ADA.[77] The former of these Acts, HIPAA, sets standards for the protection of medical information regarding natural persons and any health information and applies to healthcare program within the public health care service or any organizations involved in wellness and healthcare. HIPAA Act also sets national standards for protecting individuals' medical records and other personal health information and those health care providers that conduct certain health care transactions electronically. The Act requires appropriate safeguarding methods to protect the privacy of personal health information and sets out limits and conditions on the uses and disclosures that can be made of such information without the patient's authorization. The Act also specifies patients' rights regarding their health information, including rights to examine and obtain a copy of their health records, and to request corrections.[78] Although the Act does not apply directly to employers, it has an important function in adjusting sponsored and implemented health programs to the work environment, supported and provided by employers. Those programs often include prizes, premiums, and health insurance discounts based on staff activity and participation in the program and the level of involvement.[79] Many of such programs announced in the US, which require using devices such as smart clothing, provide rewards based on scores achieved during all sorts of activity, i.e., the number of steps climbed or the level of the user's performance, etc. Altogether, such programs are referred to as protection programs based on the user's biomedical information. In accordance with the HIPAA provisions, they have to meet a number of requirements. One of the examples is that the employer who introduces them has to provide the staff members who decide not to participate in the fitness tracking program, or are unable to join due to any sort of disabilities, with an alternative to reach an equal standard for reward.[80]

---

76 Health Insurance Portability and Accountability Act of 1996: http://www.hhs.gov/sites/default/files/ocr/privacy/hipaa/administrative/combined/hipaa-simplification-201303.pdf, last accessed 07.04.2018.
77 Americans with Disabilities Act of 1990: https://www.ada.gov/pubs/adastatute08.pdf, last accessed 07.04.2018.
78 Health Insurance Portability and Accountability Act of 1996; The Privacy Rule 45 CFR Part 160 and Subparts A and E of Part 164: http://www.hhs.gov/hipaa/for-professionals/privacy/, last accessed 07.04.2018.
79 M. Langley, *Hide your health: addressing the new privacy problem of consumer wearables*, Georgetown Law Journal, August 2015, WESTLAW™ International, p. 4.
80 A. Bevitt, H. Swan, *Challenges with the workplace…*, p. 3.

The latter Act, ADA, was passed by the United States of America Congress in 1990, with subsequent amendments, as a law regulating the protection of citizens against any sort of discrimination that could derive from their disabilities. As stated before, implementing *wearable technology* in the work environment, due to its characteristics, functions, and methods of use, could result in the discrimination against some groups of employees. To avoid such a situation or accusations of generating circumstances promoting inequity, the use of those devices is also regulated under the auspices of ADA.[81]

To sum up, as in the case of any kind of technological development, there is a number of advantages and disadvantages related to the introduction and implementation of data collecting devices and rules accompanying them, not only in common use but also in specific fields, such as work environment. The purpose of this section of the paper was to demonstrate both the risks and chances for employers and employees alike which can result from the inevitable introduction of *wearable technology* at work.

6 Legal challenges relating to implementation of wearable technology in the medical environment

6.1 Privacy and rights to data processed by medical wearable technology

Communication with the patient's caretaker via a body-borne device connected to an application installed on a smartphone is a milestone toward upgrading patients' living conditions. It also provides an opportunity to use appropriate prophylaxis and actions toward the reduction of growth of cancer cells or other diseases, which can create chances of improving life conditions. Nonetheless, it has to be pointed out that applying any novelties to a discipline as complex as medicine requires extra caution and attention paid to its legal aspects.

One of the more illustrative examples of medical wearable technology is a wrist band designed by a start-up Empatica Inc.[82] It has been designed to notify the wearer (and also his or her caretaker) about an upcoming epileptic attack.[83] Another device worth mentioning is a wristband designed to fight depression. Created in the same start-up, it is used to measure sympathetic nervous system

---

[81] Americans with Disabilities Act of 1990: https://www.ada.gov/pubs/adastatute08.pdf, last accessed 07.04.2018.

[82] https://www.empatica.com, last accessed 07.04.2018.

[83] J. Steenhuysen, *Beyond Fitbit…*, p. 1.

arousal and to recognize features related to stress, engagement, and excitement. Other wearable devices could be used to monitor conditions relating to diabetes, insomnia, obesity, or cardiac problems. Last but not least, it is worth mentioning *TheITBra*,[84] a bra with built-in sensors measuring skin temperature, allowing for a very quick discovery of breast cancer cells.[85]

Unlike "classical", health-unrelated *wearable tech* devices, such as fitness trackers, smart watches etc., devices that are designed to be used for medical purposes have to be approved by the US Food and Drug Administration (FDA)[86] to enter the market. This visibly sets them apart from other smart devices and at the same time is a step toward improved standards of producing and designing such technologies.[87] To start with, obtaining FDA's consent to introduce a medical smart device to the market is only possible after proving that a particular device is capable of objectively helping the patient, considering the type of their disease. The idea of such a requirement was very often criticized by the entrepreneurs interested in producing and designing medical smart devices. Nonetheless, after analyzing the procedures of obtaining consent, it was pointed out that devices having such an accreditation will be more desired by potential clients, will bring relatively higher income, and will protect their producers from the legal point of view. Such protection will extend to potential trials, which can be a consequence of an ineffective therapy.[88] It should be noted, though, that according to the FDA requirements, in order to obtain its consent to introduce a new medical device to the market, it is necessary not only to regulate the method of collecting personal data, but the data analysis methods will have to be thoroughly prepared, designed, and regulated in such a way that the outcome will objectively influence the knowledge about the patients' health. According to the prevailing view, the means of collecting data are very advanced, yet data analysis

---

[84] https://www.mdtmag.com/blog/2015/03/top-5-medical-devices-sxsw-2015.
[85] S. Peppet, *Regulating the Internet of Things: First Steps Towards Managing Discrimination, Privacy, Security and Consent*, Texas Law Review, 93(85), p. 102.
[86] U.S. Food and Drug Administration; The FDA is organized into the Office of the Commissioner and four directorates overseeing the core functions of the agency: Medical Products and Tobacco, Foods, Global Regulatory Operations and Policy, and Operations: http://www.fda.gov/AboutFDA/CentersOffices/OC/default.htm, last accessed 07.04.2018.
[87] J. Kasher, *Technology advances to spark clinical trial revolution*, Guide to Good Clinical Practice Newsletter, January 2014, WESTLAW™ International, p. 2.
[88] J. Steenhuysen, *Beyond Fitbit...*, p. 2.

and the ability to transfer the analyzed information into medical support still remains a challenge.[89]

Apart from these observations, the introduction of this new kind of devices to the market will obviously provide an impulse to the creation and implementation of new regulations, covering insurance plans and methods for claiming damages. On one hand, that will broaden the insurance companies' interests spectrum because the field in which they operate will become wider. This is because the insurance plans will have to cover patients specifically using medical smart devices. On the other hand, patients will have to be insured in case of any health damage potentially caused by the devices and also against harmful and inappropriate use of data analysis and a resulting inappropriate use of collected information.

In discussions on the idea of legal protection over using *wearable technology* for medical purposes in the US, attention has to be drawn to the regulations of *Patient Protection and Affordable Care Act*.[90] This Act regulates legal affairs related to financing medical care and gives doctors and other medical caretakers a tool for financing medical care. However, it needs to be noted that this regulation relates to patients that are hospitalized. There is no parallel solution that would regulate the situation of patients' using devices such as medical *wearable technology* for treatment outside hospitals or other medical units and without the direct help of those units' staff members.[91]

In the context of the European legal order, it needs to be stated at the beginning that data generated and collected by *wearable tech* devices and related to health issues are data related to the most personal and intimate areas of users' lives. What is more, quite often, such devices are able to analyze users' personality features as well. The aforementioned personal data, in accordance with most of the European regulations (not only 94/46/EC Directive[92] but also other, more specific health-related legal acts), can be processed for the purpose of analytics and observation only after meeting stringent prerequisites and levels of data protection. Because of that, the consent to their processing has to be expressed literally, in a detailed and precise way, with a very strong emphasis on its conscious

---

89 A. Thierer, *The Internet of things…*, pp. 26–27.
90 Patient Protection and Affordable Care Act: https://www.gpo.gov/fdsys/pkg/BILLS-111hr3590enr/pdf/BILLS-111hr3590enr.pdf, last accessed 07.04.2018.
91 J. Steenhuysen, *Beyond Fitbit…*, p. 2.
92 European Parliament and Council Directive 95/46/EC of 24 October 1995 on the protection of individuals with regard to the processing of personal data and on the free movement of such data [Official Journal L 281 of 23.11.1995].

statement. What is more, both the purpose of data collection and analysis and their recipient have to be clearly identified, preferably by emphasizing that the data or the final outcome of the analysis will not be processed by anybody but the device user. An exception to this rule was stated in Article 7 (f) of the Directive. It includes jurisdictional reasoning regarding the breach of privacy policy toward personal data processing, stating that "personal data may be processed only if: (f) processing is necessary for the purposes of the legitimate interests pursued by the controller or by the third party or parties to whom the data are disclosed, except where such interests are overridden by the interests for fundamental rights and freedoms of the data subject which require protection under Article 1 (1)."[93] By virtue of those restrictions, medical *wearable technology* can often be subject to exceptions whereby using and processing collected or generated data will be justified by the user's/patients well-being or health condition.

Another aspect of the legal challenge of the introduction of *wearables* to the medical market is that sometimes *wearables* can interfere with the privacy of third, unrelated parties. For instance, smart glasses supporting visually impaired people work constantly in the mode of recording the environment, processing recorded data, and communicating what is happening in the user's surroundings. That obviously includes passing some information about strangers. The concept trying to address these challenges is called *Privacy by design*[94] and it will finally find its recognition in the upcoming GDPR regulation. It means that each new service or business process that makes use of personal data must take the protection of third parties into consideration. An organization needs to be able to show that they have adequate security measures in place and that compliance is monitored.[95] The device has to have a visible feature showing that it is currently operating in the data-collecting mode, so that all members of the environment can register the fact of such devices' being used. This rule was introduced in the proposal of the GDPR: Article 25 includes data protection by design and by

---

93 Article 7(f) European Parliament and Council Directive 95/46/EC of 24 October 1995 on the protection of individuals with regard to the processing of personal data and on the free movement of such data [Official Journal L 281 of 23.11.1995: http://eur-lex.europa.eu/LexUriServ/LexUriServ.do?uri=CELEX:31995L0046:en:HTML, last accessed 07.04.2018.

94 A. Cavoukian, *Embed Privacy – by Design, or Risk Losing Privacy Forever*, Berkeley Center for Law & Technology March 11, 2016, https://www.law.berkeley.edu/wp-content/uploads/2016/03/Ann-Cavoukian.pdf.

95 http://www.eudataprotectionregulation.com/#!data-protection-design-by-default/c20k7, last accessed 07.04.2018.

default requirements.⁹⁶ The latter of the terms cited should be defined as a concept where *Privacy by Default* simply means that the strictest privacy settings automatically apply once a customer acquires a new product or service. In other words, no manual change to the privacy settings should be required from the user. There is also a temporal element to this principle, as personal information must by default be kept for the amount of time necessary to provide the product or service.⁹⁷

To recapitulate, this law will require the existence of a data controller, responsible for data flows in the *wearables* environment, to be able to show that adequate security levels are in place and that compliance is monitored. In practice, this means that an IT department of a technology producing or distributing company must take privacy into account during the whole life cycle of the system or process development.⁹⁸

6.2 Product liability and safety of use

The more serious the scope of devices operation is, the more risk during the process of using it is generated, which is mainly the case of devices designed to control or support people's health. The same rule applies to medical *wearable technology*. Some of them can seriously harm the patients' health conditions if not used properly or due to some technical deficiencies that may occur regardless of the user's actions, both when they start operating and while used long-term. To give an example, let us consider a device that is supposed to measure glucose levels in the patients' blood and dose insulin to the veins of a person suffering from diabetes. If the measurement is not executed accurately or insulin is released in an inadequate dose, the life or health of the patient can be put at major risk.

This is why another important issue related to medical *wearable tech* has to be legally regulated. First of all, if a device does not work properly, usually the first, automatic reaction is to switch it off and turn it back on. However, when it comes to *wearable tech*, the most obvious reaction is not the easiest one as, e.g.,

---

96 Article 23 of the Regulation of the European Parliament and of the Council on the protection of individuals with regard to the processing of personal data and on the free movement of such data: http://eur-lex.europa.eu/legal-content/EN/TXT/PDF/?uri=CELEX:52012PC0011&from=EN, last accessed 07.04.2018.
97 Privacy by default: http://www.eudataprotectionregulation.com/#!data-protection-design-by-default/c20k7, last accessed 07.04 2018.
98 D. Schartum, *Making Privacy by Design Operative*. International Journal of Law and Information Technology, 2016, 24(2), pp. 151–175.

it is not always possible to undress in public. What is more, the *wearables* definition implies that those devices are supposed to constantly operate in the standby mode, which is why turning them off and on is not an option. Nevertheless, that issue is rather easy to handle by means of installing the emergency mode, ready to operate when the device is not fully adjusted to work properly, without any harm to the patient's health.[99]

The purpose of using devices such as medical *wearable technology* is supposed to spare the user the necessity to constantly control some of the activities related to healthcare (i.e., medicine dosing). On one hand, this is the aim of using such devices: to improve patients' living conditions. On the other, when it comes to issues as serious as health, controlling medicine dosage each time seems inevitable. The method to overcome this barrier without, at the same time, defeating the purpose of medical *wearables* is to include an alarm feature in the device, which notifies the patient or their caretakers that the substance is being administered to the former's system and requests that the patient himself or the caretaker accept that action. If this solution is applied, safety rules will not be breached and, at the same time, the devices features can be intact.[100]

6.3 Medical wearable technology – legal qualification

The European legal framework for smart clothing used for medical purposes requires qualifying those devices as medicinal or medical, so they can to be governed by existing legal acts. *Wearable devices,* used for treatment or health supporting purposes, belong to the other category. They can be defined as products including instruments, devices, operating systems, or other objects or substances used directly for medical purposes but their use cannot be qualified as using a medicinal product.[101] At the same time, there is no need for such devices to have direct contact with human body to be considered a medical device. In that context, medical, not medicinal devices aim to:

- recognize, prevent, survey, treat, or alleviate diseases; or
- recognize, survey, treat, alleviate, or compensate injuries or disabilities; or
- examine or change the anatomic structure, replace parts of the anatomic structure, or examine, change, or replace a physiological process.[102]

---

99   J. Steenhuysen, *Beyond Fitbit…*, p. 2.
100 K. Khachaturian, *Medical Device Regulation in the Information Age: A Mobile Health Perspective*, Jurimetrics Journal, Summer 2015, WESTLAW™ International, p. 4.
101 R. Mathys, *Legal…*, pp. 23–24.
102 *Ibidem*, pp. 24–25.

Most of the devices, qualified as smart clothing that corresponds with the aforementioned criteria, and whose operations allow the outlined measurements, can be called medical devices.

Unlike medicinal products, medical devices do not have to pass the official authorization procedure to be introduced to the market. They still have to meet the safety, risk assessment, adjustment procedure, import, export, and advertising actions requirements. Those are based on the producers' and distributors' responsibility procedures. Before admitting a new device to official trading, it has to be approved and authorized as safe and adequate for its purpose. Depending on a type of device, the authorization has to be conducted either by an external state-accredited body or internally, by the producer itself.[103] After a successful authorization by an adequate body, and after establishing that the product is fit for introduction to the market, it has to be marked with the "'CE" sign (Conformité Européenne),[104] which confirms that the item meets the applicable E.U. directives' requirements.

The current legal framework relevant to the discussed scope was formed back in the 1990s and due to its obsolescence in view of technical and technological development it cannot always apply to current requirements of the market of modern devices, after more than 20 years after the implementation. The idea to change it for medical smart devices was proposed and was to be enforced in 2014, but this is yet to happen. The idea includes the concept to regulate products that are designed to be injected or invasive, and can be applied without a clear medical purpose if they carry negligible risk of injury (like e.g., contact lenses).[105] With a proper phrasing of any potential acts of that kind, there is a very high possibility that this framework could include medical *wearable devices* and regulate their use.

To conclude, it is worth mentioning the subject already outlined during the discussion of *wearables* in the workplace. Regarding their preventive purposes and the possibility to use them for the purpose of preventing injuries, damage, or any other health-related risks, the issue of insurance is important. At the moment, it is impossible for any insurance company, based on either the European or American legal framework, to decide about the compensation in the case of injury or about the health insurance contribution rate based on the use of health-supporting technology. Under *Patient Protection and Affordable*

---

103 *Ibidem*, p. 26.
104 https://ec.europa.eu/growth/single-market/ce-marking_en, last accessed 07.08.2018.
105 A. Thierer, *The Internet of things…*, p. 23.

Care Act[106] in the US legal framework, it is not possible to introduce for a group of users a healthcare program based on *wearable technology* applications that would justify the reduction of health insurance contributions. Despite that, according to PricewaterhouseCoopers LLP, it is only a matter of time before technology reaches such a level of development that regulating it will be crucial in all legal frameworks.[107]

As a conclusion, it will be emphasized that including *wearable tech* in the process of protecting and supporting patients' health or treatment is not inevitable yet. However, in view of surveys conducted, with the possible outcomes of developing such devices, it appears that we are witnessing ground-breaking developments in the field of health protection, health care, and treating diseases considered incurable to date.

---

106 Patient Protection and Affordable Care Act: https://www.gpo.gov/fdsys/pkg/BILLS-111hr3590enr/pdf/BILLS-111hr3590enr.pdf, last accessed 07.04.2018.

107 *The Future of Wearables*, Consumer Intelligence Series; PricewaterhouseCoopers LLP: http://www.pwc.com/us/en/retail-consumer/publications/assets/pwc-cis-wearable-future.pdf, last accessed 07.04.2018.

Dagmara Jaroszewska-Choraś and Sebastian Sykuna

Selected Legal Regulations Concerning Biometrics and the Biometric Data[1]

1 Introduction

The dynamic developments in the area of information technologies can influence the sphere of human rights and freedoms. Citizens' right to privacy and to the protection of their personal data may be infringed by those technologies. One such technology is automated biometric human identification. Biometrics (or biometric human identification) has now been researched for over 100 years. The first studies in the field concerned fingerprints, whichare now a popular biometric modality. However, other modalities have also emerged over the last decades, such as face recognition, hand geometry, and hand veins geometry among others. Biometric techniques allow for human identification on the basis of human physiological or behavioral characteristics. Therefore, there are some concerns about biometric techniques used for the surveillance and monitoring of societies.

Biometrics is also used by organizations working on broadly understood homeland security. Prüm Decision[2] is an example of a legal regulation allowing for the processing of information from fingerprints and DNA profiles for counterterrorism purposes. It regulates transborder exchange of DNA profiles, fingerprints, vehicle registration data, and the information about suspects in planning terrorist attacks. However, those regulations are beyond the scope of this paper.

The major goal of this paper is the analysis of biometrics in the context of current and forthcoming regulations concerning personal data protection. Selected national legal frameworks for personal data protection will be compared and evaluated, namely those from Slovakia, Slovenia, and Czech Republic. Those countries were selected due to the fact that not in all the member countries

---

1   This paper is based and uses material from the book: D. Jaroszewska-Choraś, *Biometria – aspekty prawne*, Gdańsk 2016. Legal status of this chapter is for 1 December 2017.
2   Council Decision 2008/615/JHA of 23 June 2008 on the stepping up of cross-border cooperation, particularly in combating terrorism and cross-border crime, Official Journal of the European Union, L 210, 06.08.2008, pp. 1–11.

the aspects related to biometric data protection are regulated. The selected countries are, on the other hand, good examples of positive changes with respect to biometric data protection. It is worth adding that such issues are also regulated by law in Italy and Luxembourg, but the relevant acts are not as precise and detailed as in Slovenia or Slovakia.

Furthermore, the authors will also discuss two more statutes, namely legal acts from the United States and from the United Kingdom. The American federal *Biometric Identifier Privacy Act* was introduced in New Jersey.[3] It contains detailed provisions regarding biometrics and biometric data. In the United Kingdom, *Protection of Freedoms Act* (PFA) was introduced in 2012. It contains many innovative provisions regulating the use of biometric technologies.

2 Fundamental concepts of biometrics

Before analyzing the legal aspects, the term "biometrics" should be explained. It originates from Greek, where *bios* means "life" and *metron* means "to measure." Therefore, biometrics is understood as measurements for automated human identification or verification. Biometrics is a science for identification and verification of people on the basis of their physiological and behavioral characteristics.[4]

Recognition of human beings, in other words confirming their identity, is a very important task of many computer systems. So far, human identity has been usually confirmed by such means as documents, credentials, and Personal Identification Numbers (PINs). However, nowadays, biometric technologies have been attracting interest and attention. Those techniques rely on the digital measuring of some physiological or behavioral characteristics, building feature vectors, and comparing them to previously enrolled templates. It is worth mentioning that some systems are quite natural, since in everyday life humans recognize each other by biometric means, such as examining faces or hearing voices, rather than by some special numbers such as PIN.[5]

---

3   *Biometric Identifier Privacy Act*, Assembly, No. 2448, State of New Jersey, 210th Legislature, Introduced June 13, 2002.

4   D. Jaroszewska-Choraś, *Biometria – aspekty prawne*, Gdańsk 2016, p. 28; Jasiński, *Zagadnienia biometrii w Unii Europejskiej, Materiały Robocze 4 (8)/06*, Centrum Europejskie – Natolin, Warszawa 2006, p. 8; K. Krasowski, I. Sołtyszewski, *Biometria – zarys problematyki*, Problemy Kryminalistyki 2006, no 252, p. 39.

5   C. Shoniregun, S. Crosier, *Securing Biometrics Applications*, Springer, Heidelberg 2007, p. 49.

There are two classes of biometric modalities: physiological (also termed as anatomical) and behavioral.[6] Physiological characteristics include fingerprints, palmprints, hand geometry, face recognition, etc. Examples of behavioral modalities are voice recognition, gait, keystroke dynamics, signatures etc.

Biometrics is gaining popularity since the traditional methods have some disadvantages: it is easy to lose keys and ID cards, it is difficult to remember all the passwords and PINs, etc.[7] Moreover, in essence, traditional methods are based on something that a person possesses or remembers (has to know),[8] so in reality those methods do not identify a person himself/herself.[9] On the other hand, biometric methods identify humans and their unique characteristics.

The term "biometric data" can be defined as biological properties, behavioral aspects, physiological characteristics, living traits, or repeatable actions, both unique to an individual and measurable, even if the patterns used in practice to technically measure them involve a certain degree of probability.[10]

Biometric data should be treated and understood as special data, since such data directly describe physiological or behavioral characteristics of a given person and allow for direct identification.[11] Typical examples of biometric data are fingerprints, iris or retina patterns, voice, hand geometry, as well as performing such actions as walking, writing signatures, typing on a keyboard etc. Biometric data can be considered as an intermediary between information and a particular person. Biometric data can be understood as identifiers and are used to establish the identity of a given person.

---

6 R. Bolle, J. Connell, S. Pankanti, N. Ratha, A. Senior, *Biometria*, Warszawa 2008, p. XXIX.
7 A. Jain, A. Ross, *Introduction to Biometrics*, [in:] A. K. Jain, P. Flynn, A. Ross (eds.), *Handbook of Biometrics*, Springer, New York 2008, p. 1.
8 L. Hong, A. Jain, *Integrating Faces and Fingerprints for Personal Identification*, IEEE Transactions on Pattern Analysis and Machine Intelligence, vol. 20, no 12, 1998, p. 1295.
9 A. Jain, *Biometric Recognition: How Do I Know Who You Are*, [in:] Kalviainen et al. (eds.), SCIA, LNCS 2540, 2005, p. 1.
10 Article 29 Data Protection Working Party, Opinion 3/2012 *on developments in biometric technologies*, adopted on 27th April 2012, 00720/12/EN,WP 193, p. 4. It is worth noting that this Working Party was set up under Article 29 of Directive 95/46/EC. It is an independent European advisory body on data protection and privacy. Its tasks are described in Article 30 of Directive 95/46/EC and Article 15 of Directive 2002/58/EC.
11 Article 29 Data Protection Working Party,*Working document on biometrics*, adopted on 1st August 2003, 12168/02/EN, WP 80, p. 2.

Very often, words such as "identification," "verification," and "recognition" are used as synonyms. However, from a technical point of view, recognition is a much wider term, which includes two possible modes of the biometric system operation, namely identification and verification, whichare not the same[12].

The identification of an individual by a biometric system is typically the process of comparing biometric data of an individual to a number of biometric templates stored in a database (i.e., a one-to-many matching process).[13]

The verification of an individual by a biometric system is typically the process of comparing the biometric data of an individual to a single biometric template stored in a device (i.e., a one-to-one matching process).[14]

Biometrics, however, cannot be considered as a solely technological issue. We need to discuss, and remember about, its potential influence on fundamental human rights, privacy, personal data protection, and human dignity. Therefore, in the remainder of this paper, we focus on the legal aspects and regulations of biometrics and biometric data.

3 Biometric data protection in European and international law

Nowadays, the legal aspects of biometrics are formally regulated as far as the application of law by public institutions is concerned. For example, legal provisions concerning biometric techniques in travel documents are in place. It is worth noticing that Council Regulation (EC) No 2252/2004 on standards for security features and biometrics in passports and travel documents issued by Member States was passed on 13 December 2004.[15] This act came into force on 18 January 2015. Then, it was amended by Regulation (EC) No 444/2009 of the European Parliament and of the Council of 28 May 2009 amending Council Regulation (EC) No 2252/2004 on standards for security features and biometrics in passports and travel documents issued by Member States.[16]

---

12 D. Jaroszewska-Choraś, *Biometria – aspekty prawne*, Gdańsk 2016, *Supra* note 6, p. 29.
13 R. Bolle, J. Connell, S. Pankanti, N. Ratha, A. Senior, *Biometria*, p. 12; L. Hong, A. Jain, *Integrating Faces and Fingerprints for Personal Identification IEEE Transactions on Pattern Analysis and Machine Intelligence* 1998, vol. 20, no 12, p. 1296.
14 R. Bolle, J. Connell, S. Pankanti, N. Ratha, A. Senior, *Biometria*, p. 13; A. Jain, A. Ross, *Introduction…*,p. 6; L. Hong, A. Jain., *Integrating Faces…*, p. 1296.
15 Official Journal of the European Union, L 385, 29.12.2004, pp. 1–6.
16 Official Journal of the European Union, L 142, 06.06.2009, pp. 1–4.

Moreover, there exist information systems processing the personal and biometric data of refugees, asylum seekers, and those applying for a visa. The most important systems areVisa Information System (VIS) and Second generation Schengen Information System (SISII). For example, VIS allows Schengen States to exchange visa-related data. It consists of a central IT system and a communications infrastructure, which links this central system to national systems. VIS connects consulates in non-European Union (EU) countries and all external border-crossing points of Schengen States. It processes data and decisions relating to applications for short-stay visas to visit, or to transit through, the Schengen Area. The system can perform biometric matching, primarily of fingerprints, for identification and verification purposes.[17]

One of the most important examples of an IT system using and processing biometric data for identifying refugees and asylum seekers was the creation of a database called Eurodac.[18] Eurodac is a system for European Dactyloscopy. This database was created under the Dublin Convention of 1990. This convention introduced the provision that each asylum application is to be processed in only one EU member country.[19]

Eurodac started operating on 15 January 2003. New statutes regulating the operation of the Eurodac system were introduced on 26 June 2013.[20] They

---

17 http://ec.europa.eu/ (last accessed 27.11.2017).
18 Eurodac was introduced by Council Regulation (EC) No 2725/2000 of 11 December 2000 concerning the establishment of 'Eurodac' for the comparison of fingerprints for the effective application of the Dublin Convention, Official Journal of the European Union, L 316, 15.12.2000, pp. 1–10. However, the operational provisions are included in the Council Regulation (EC) No 407/2002 of 28 February 2002 laying down certain rules to implement Regulation (EC) No 2725/2000 concerning the establishment of 'Eurodac' for the comparison of fingerprints for the effective application of the Dublin Convention, Official Journal of the European Union, L 62, 05.03.2002, pp. 1–6.
19 Official Journal of the European Union, C 254, 19.08.1997 r., pp.1–12. The convention was then replaced by Council Regulation (EC) No 343/2003 of 18 February 2003 establishing the criteria and mechanisms for determining the Member State responsible for examining an asylum application lodged in one of the Member States by a third-country national, Official Journal of the European Union, L 50, 25.02.2003, pp. 1–10 (called Dublin II). Then Council Regulation (EC) No 343/2003 was replaced by the Council and European Parliament Regulation (EC) No 604/2013.
20 Regulation (EU) No 603/2013 of the European Parliament and of the Council of 26 June 2013 on the establishment of 'Eurodac' for the comparison of fingerprints for the effective application of Regulation (EU) No 604/2013 establishing the criteria and mechanisms for determining the Member State responsible for examining an application for international protection lodged in one of the Member States by a third-country

significantly changed the original purposes for which the system was developed. New regulations came into force on 20 July 2015. Until then, Council Regulation 2725/2000 had been used.[21]

In the European Union law, international public law, and national laws, there are many legal guarantees pertaining to the protection of personal data and of the right to privacy, the main ones being:

- European Convention for the Protection of Human Rights and Fundamental Freedoms,[22]
- Directive 95/46/EC of 24 October 1995 on the protection of individuals with regard to the processing of personal data and on the free movement of such data,[23]
- Regulation (EU) 2016/679 of the European Parliament and the Council of 27 April 2016 on the protection of natural persons with regard to the processing of personal data and on the free movement of such data, and repealing Directive 95/46/EC (General Data Protection Regulation),[24]
- Convention for the Protection of Individuals with regard to Automatic Processing of Personal Data (Convention No. 108),[25]
- Charter of Fundamental Rights of the European Union,[26]
- International Covenant on Civil and Political Rights[27] and

---

national or a stateless person and on requests for the comparison with Eurodac data by Member States' law enforcement authorities and Europol for law enforcement purposes, and amending Regulation (EU) No 1077/2011 establishing a European Agency for the operational management of large-scale IT systems in the area of freedom, security and justice, Official Journal of the European Union, L 180, 29.06.2013, pp. 1–30.

21 Council Regulation (EC) No 2725/2000 of 11 December 2000 concerning the establishment of 'Eurodac' for the comparison of fingerprints for the effective application of the Dublin Convention, Official Journal of the European Communities, L 316, 15.12.2000, pp. 1–10.
22 B. Gronowska, T. Jasudowicz, C. Mik, *Prawa człowieka. Wybór dokumentów międzynarodowych*, Toruń 1999, p. 83.
23 Official Journal L 281, 23.11.1995, pp. 31–50.
24 Official Journal of the European Union, L 319, 04.05.2016, pp. 1–88. The regulation will come into force on 25 May 2018. It is worth noting that it will replace the Directive 95/46/EC.
25 Opening for signature in Strasbourg on 28.01.1981.
26 Official Journal of the European Union, C 326, 26.10.2012, pp. 391–407.
27 A. Przyborowska-Klimczak, *Prawo międzynarodowe publiczne. Wybór dokumentów*, Lublin 2005, pp. 172–192.

- OECD Guidelines on the Protection of Privacy and Transborder Flows of Personal Data OECD.[28]

The human right to privacy and personal data protection is, therefore, protected by international and European (EU) law. Moreover, some aspects of the relation of biometrics to personal data protection and the right to privacy have been discussed in many documents, opinions, and reports.[29]

It should be emphasized that Directive 95/46/EC and Council of Europe Convention No. 108 do not contain specific provisions relating tobiometric data or biometrics.[30] Although the term "biometrics" does not appear in the Directive and in the Convention, it may be concluded from the contents of the provisions in the above acts that the processing of biometric data requires "acquiring, transmitting, processing, recording and storage of the sound or image data related to individuals." Therefore, both the Directive and the Convention apply to the processing that requires such data[31].

Moreover, it cannot be forgotten that biometric data constitute a special category of personal data.

Data are personal once it is possible to identify a person whom the data concern (as in art. 2a of Convention 108 and point 1.2 of the OECD Guidelines).

---

28 OECD *Guidelines on the Protection of Privacy and Transborder Flows of Personal Data*, Paris, OECD, 1980.
29 See Article 29 Data Protection Working Party; Opinion 3/2005 *on Implementing the Council Regulation (EC) No 2252/2004 of 13 December 2004 on standards for security features and biometrics in passports and travel documents issued by Member States*, WP 112, Adopted on 30th September 2005; Consultative Committee of the Convention for the Protection of Individuals with regard to automatic processing of personal data, *Progress report on the application of the principles of Convention 108 to the collection and processing of biometric data*, 2005.
30 The issues related to biometric data have been regulated among others in the Council Regulation (EC) No 2252/2004 of 13 December 2004 on standards for security features and biometrics in passports and travel documents issued by Member States, Official Journal of the European Union, L 385, 29.12.2004, pp. 1–6; changes to the regulation have been introduced in Regulation (EC) No 444/2009 of the European Parliament and of the Council of 28 May 2009 amending Council Regulation (EC) No 2252/2004 on standards for security features and biometrics in passports and travel documents issued by Member State (Official Journal of the European Union, L 142, 06.06.2009, pp. 1–4).
31 D. Jaroszewska-Choraś, *Biometria – aspekty prawne*, Gdańsk 2016, *Supra* note 6, p. 87–88.

The evaluation of the nature of data should be performed by each organization processing data.[32]

Some guidance on this can be found in paragraph 26 of the preamble to Directive 95/45/EC. Therein, it is stated that the principles of data protection must apply to any information concerning an identified or identifiable person. In order to determine whether a person is identifiable, all the ways should be considered which the administrator of the data or any other person can use to identify a given person. If data are anonymous, the principles of data protection do not apply to them. The provisions of the directive do not, therefore, apply to personal data (biometric data), which are anonymous.

The application of biometric technologies in order to establish identities requires the processing of a special category of personal data, namely biometric data. The processing of such data has to be performed in accordance with legal regulations concerning personal data protection. The most important rules concern proportionality, fairness, lawfulness, legitimacy, and purposiveness.

The crucial aspects of processing biometric data can be found in points 14 and 15 of the preamble to Directive 95/45/EC. Point 14 stipulates as follows: "Whereas, given the importance of the developments under way, in the framework of the information society, of the techniques used to capture, transmit, manipulate, record, store or communicate sound and image data relating to natural persons, this Directive should be applicable to processing involving such data."[33] Point 15 stipulates as follows: "Whereas the processing of such data is covered by this Directive only if it is automated or if the data processed are contained or are intended to be contained in a filing system structured according to specific criteria relating to individuals, so as to permit easy access to the personal data in question."

Biometric data (in the form of images or sounds) are collected, registered, and transmitted, and their processing can be fully automated. Biometric dataare personal data, so they have to be acquired and processed in accordance with the provisions of the Directive, since such data allow for the identification of a given person.[34]

---

32 X. Konarski, *Internet i prawo w praktyce*, Warszawa 2002, pp. 113–116.
33 P. de Hert, *Biometrics: legal issues and implication*, p. 13, http://www.statewatch.org/news/2005/apr/jrc-biometrics-paul-de-hert.pdf. (last accessed 27.11.2017).
34 D. Choraś, *Biometrics and Data Protection* in: A. Mitas (ed.), *Biometrics – 2010. Monograph*, Gliwice 2011, p. 37.

The terms related to biometrics and to biometric data can be found in documents whichare the so-called soft law, e.g., in the opinions of the Working Party on Article 29 on the Protection of Personal Data. In one of the documents published in 2003, it established several rules and guidelines, and noted the crucial role of the rule of proportionality.[35] Furthermore, the Consultative Committee of Convention 108 also commented on the application of this rule to biometric technologies.[36]

Another fundamental requirement for processing personal data is the need to comply with the rules and the law (legality).[37] However, in the context of the processing of personal data in biometric systems, the rules of proportionality and purposiveness are also crucial.

The proportionality test should check if the purpose of the processing of such data cannot be achieved by other, less invasive (than biometric) means, which would not infringe on or limit the right to privacy.

According to Article 6 of Directive 95/46/EC, personal data must be collected for specified, explicit, and legitimate purposes and not further processed in a way incompatible with those purposes. In addition, personal data must be adequate, relevant, and not excessive in relation to the purposes for which they are collected and further processed (purpose principle).

Further processing of data for historical, statistical, and scientific purposes is not illegal on condition that the Member States ensure appropriate security means.[38] Similar statements with regard to biometric data

---

35 See: Article 29 Data Protection Working Party; Opinion 3/2005 *on Implementing the Council Regulation (EC) No 2252/2004 of 13 December 2004 on standards for security features and biometrics in passports and travel documents issued by Member States*, WP 112, Adopted on 30th September 2005, p. 9.

36 *Progress report on the application of the principles of Convention 108 to the collection and processing of biometric data (2005)*, p. 18.

37 For more details see: M. Jagielski, *Prawo do ochrony danych osobowych. Standardy europejskie*, Warszawa 2010, pp. 78–87.

38 According to point 28 of the Directive 95/46/EC: "Whereas any processing of personal data must be lawful and fair to the individuals concerned; whereas, in particular, the data must be adequate, relevant and not excessive in relation to the purposes for which they are processed; whereas such purposes must be explicit and legitimate and must be determined at the time of collection of the data; whereas the purposes of processing further to collection shall not be incompatible with the purposes as they were originally specified".

processing can be found in Article 5 of Convention 108[39] and in the OECD Guidelines.[40]

According to the opinion of Article 29 Data Protection Working Party, also additional aspects have to be considered in the course of processing biometric data.[41] Those aspects concern the lawfulness and fairness of data processing. The processing of biometric data must be based on the grounds of legitimacy provided for in Article 7 of Directive 95/46/EC.[42] However, in the case of sensitive data processing, such processing has to be compliant with the provisions mentioned in Article 8 of the Directive. Article 29 Data Protection Working Partyalso stated that in the case of biometric data processing the central data storage of data for authentication should be avoided. It is a fact that the centralized storage of biometric data is inevitable for identification, but in this case the principle of proportionality should be applied.[43] The processing of biometric data in large centralized databases carries the risk of the infringement of the right to privacy and personal data protection because of the potentially harmful effects in relation to the persons whose dataare processed.[44] The purpose and the principle of proportionality should be applied to biometrics. According to the provisions of

---

39 According to point 28 of the Convention: Personal data undergoing automatic processing shall be:
a. obtained and processed fairly and lawfully; b. stored for specified and legitimate purposes and not used in a way incompatible with those purposes; c. adequate, relevant and not excessive in relation to the purposes for which they are stored; d. accurate and, where necessary, kept up to date; e. preserved in a form which permits identification of the data subjects for no longer than is required for the purpose for which those data are stored.
40 Points 8, 9, 10 of the OECD Guidelines.
41 Article 29 Data Protection Working Party, *Working document on biometrics*, WP 80, 1.08.2003, p. 8.
42 For more details see: M. Jagielski, *op. cit.*, pp. 81–87; M. Polok, *Bezpieczeństwo danych osobowych*, Warszawa 2008, pp. 90–94. See also: Article 29 Data Protection Working Party, Opinion 3/2012 *on developments in biometric technologies*, adopted on 27th April 2012, pp. 10–13.
43 Article 29 - Data Protection Working Party, *Working document on biometrics*, 12168/02/ENWP 80, adopted on 1 August 2003, p. 6 and the following. Similar issues have been analysed in Article 29 –Data Protection Working Party, Opinion 3/2005 *on Implementing the Council Regulation (EC) No 2252/2004 of 13 December 2004 on standards for security features and biometrics in passports and travel documents issued by Member States*, 1710/05/EN-rev WP 112, adopted on 30 September 2005, p. 3.
44 Article 29 –Data Protection Working Party Opinion 3/2012 *on developments in biometric technologies*, adopted on 27th April 2012, p. 8.

Directive 95/46/EC, member states shall ensure that personal dataare processed fairly and lawfully.[45] The concept of "fairness" may mean that data processing should not unreasonably violate the privacy, independence, and integrity of a person,[46] and that it should be open. "Lawfulness," in its turn, is a concept that states that data processing should not be against the law.

It is worth emphasizing that the European legislator understands the problems with the protection of personal data, including biometric data. The answer to rapid changes in technologies is Regulation (EU) 2016/679 of the European Parliament and the Council of 27 April 2016 on the protection of natural persons with regard to the processing of personal data and on the free movement of such data, and repealing Directive 95/46/EC (General Data Protection Regulation),[47] where the notion of biometric data was defined. In accordance with the legal definition contained in Article 4 (14) of said Regulation, "biometric data means personal data resulting from specific technical processing relating to the physical, physiological or behavioural characteristics of a natural person, which allow or confirm the unique identification of that natural person, such as facial images or dactyloscopic data." In the Proposal for a Regulation of the European Parliament and of the Council on the protection of individuals with regard to the processing of personal data and on the free movement of such data (General Data Protection Regulation), the definition was stated as follows: "biometric data means any data relating to the physical, physiological or behavioural characteristics of an individual which allow their unique identification, such as facial images, or dactyloscopic data" [Article 4 (11)].

Moreover, the provisions of Regulation (EU) 2016/679 of the European Parliament and the Council of 27 April 2016 on the protection of natural persons with regard to the processing of personal data and on the free movement of such data, and repealing Directive 95/46/EC (and also in the Proposal) only address the issue of the "identification" of an individual. However, biometric systems allow for both biometric identification and biometric authentication. Furthermore, it needs to be remembered that technical sciences define biometric authentication as a process of comparing biometric data of an individual (sampled in real time during the process) with a unique biometric model stored in the device (the so-called one-to-one matching process). As a consequence, the imprecise nature

---

45 Article 6 point a of Convention No. 108 also indicates that personal data undergoing automatic processing shall be obtained and processed fairly and lawfully (art. 5a).
46 L. Bygrave, *Data Protection Law. Approaching its Rationale, Logic and Limits*, The Hague, London, New York 2002, p. 58.
47 Official Journal of the European Union, L 319, 04.05.2016, pp. 1–88.

of the provision presented in Article 4 (14) of the Regulation may cause interpretation problems in the future[48].

Of course, one can ask if such a new definition will improve the legal aspects of the processing of biometric data. However, since biometrics is more widely used in public and private sectors, it seems that a separate legal act would enable future biometric developments assuring a wider protection of human rights and privacy. Changes for the better in that respect can be observed in regulations introduced in the United States and in the United Kingdom, where aspects relevant to biometrics have been regulated in detail.

4 Legal regulations for biometric data in the United States and in the United Kingdom

After the tragic attacks on World Trade Centre of 11 September 2001, the United States have become the leader of implementing biometric technologies, e.g., in order to protect borders and give them to law enforcement agencies. Those techniques were seen as effective means for prevention of future terror acts.[49]

It is worth noting that some US states introduced legal regulations concerning biometrics. One such example is the *Biometric Identifier Privacy Act*, implemented in New Jersey.[50]

The *Biometric Identifier Privacy Act* contains detailed provisions regarding biometrics and biometric data. The legislator used the term "biometric identifier," which should be understood as biometric data. In accordance with this regulation, "biometric identifier" is a retina or iris scan, fingerprint, voiceprint, or record of hand or face geometry.[51]

According to Article 3a *Biometric Identifier Privacy Act*, "[n]otwithstanding any other provision of law to the contrary, no person shall obtain a biometric identifier of an individual, for the purpose of commercial advantage, without authorization of the individual." This provision emphasized that, in general, biometric data cannot be used for commercial purposes. However, it seems possible to use such

---

48 D. Jaroszewska-Choraś, *Biometria – aspekty prawne*, Gdańsk 2016, *Supra* note 6, p. 308.
49 The legal basis for using biometric data by federal agencies for identification of persons were Tyree legal acts: *USA Patriot Act* of 26th October 2001 (antiterrorism act), *Aviation and Transportation Security Act* of 19th November 2001and the *Enhanced Border Security and Visa Entry Reform Act of 14th May 2002*.
50 *Biometric Identifier Privacy Act*; Assembly, No. 2448, State of New Jersey, 210th Legislature, Introduced June 13, 2002.
51 Art. 2, *Biometric Identifier Privacy Act*.

data for noncommercial purposes. Therefore, in such situations, there is still a significant risk of a so-called "function creep." It means that biometric data originally collected for a particular purpose can be after some time used for another purpose.

The provisions included in the *Biometric Identifier Privacy Act* forbid the selling, leasing, and revealing of biometric identifiers by private institutions and also by governmental agencies.[52]

However, there are some exceptions to this provision. A person who possesses a biometric identifier of an individual shall not sell, lease, or otherwise disclose the biometric identifier to another person unless:

1. the individual consents to the sale, lease or disclosure;
2. the sale, lease or disclosure completes a financial transaction requested or authorized by the individual[53];
3. the sale, lease or disclosure is required or permitted by federal or State law; or
4. the sale, lease or disclosure is made by or to a law enforcement agency for a law enforcement purpose.[54]

In particular, the conditions specified in the last sentence are quite alarming. The provisions of the act do not define what is meant by protection of homeland security. It is not specified if private institutions can (of their free will) or must provide such data. Moreover, the conditions under which biometric data shall be provided to government agencies are not specified. Arethose conditions related to serious crime and terrorism, or maybe just a suspicion of such a crime is enough? Unfortunately, such a fuzzy wording of the provision can allow for too much invasion into the right of privacy. In the act, the concept of "consent" appeared, which is an important notion in the case of biometric data. However, this provision is not precise, since it gives no details on how to understand the "consent" expressed by the biometric data owner/subject. Should the consent be expressed in writing? Or is the will expressed informally enough? It seems as if no provision exists which would enforce the necessity to inform the data subjects about the possible threats and risks related to biometric data processing.

The provisions of this regulation imply that private persons and public agencies which store biometric identifiers cannot reveal these identifiers and are obliged to securely store and transmit such data in an appropriate manner.

---

52 Government agencies are defined as the country, each its agency, and employees of such agencies.
53 It should be noted that in the case of government agencies, such reasons are not specified.
54 See art. 3a and art. 4a of *Biometric Identifier Privacy Act*.

A person whose biometric data is not processed in accordance with the act can file for a compensation of 25,000 dollars for each count of the violation of the act, and also for the reimbursement of the attorney's fees.[55] Also, if the provisions regarding the use of biometric identifiers are violated by a government agency, the person can apply to the Supreme Court of the United States for relevant compensation and for the reimbursement the attorney's fees. Unlike in the case of the private sector, the upper threshold of the compensation is not specified.

The regulation under scrutiny, even though it concerns state legislation, not federal legal framework, is a very important one regarding the relation of biometrics to the law. It is an attempt to introduce provisions regulating the processing of biometric data. Those provisions are crucial in order to limit unauthorized use of biometric data.

Another interesting solution with regard to legal regulation of biometrics is the British *PFA 2012*. This regulation, introduced in the UK, should be a benchmark regulation for other European countries. It is worth mentioning that in the UK, apart from this regulation, a law devoted strictly to personal data protection is also in place, namely the *Data Protection Act of 1998*, which does not regulate biometric data protection.

The *PFA 2012* consists of several parts. The first one concerns only biometric data. The processing of biometric data is limited to two domains. The first domain is the use of such data by law enforcement agencies. The second domain is the collecting of biometric data from children in schools. The section of concerning the processing of biometric data from children is to be applied to any instance of the processing of such data by any relevant body representing the school.

It is worth noticing that before the first processing of a child's biometric information or after the coming into force of subsection the relevant authority must notify each parent of the child:

a. of its intention to process the child's biometric information, and
b. that the parent may object at any time to the processing of the information.

It is worth emphasizing that the relevant authority must ensure that a child's biometric information is not processed unless:

a. at least one parent of the child consents to the information being processed, and
b. no parent of the child has withdrawn his or her consent, or otherwise objected, to the information being processed.[56]

---

55 Art. 3e *Biometric Identifier Privacy Act*.
56 *PFA 2012*, Part 1 — Regulation of biometric data; Chapter 2 — Protection of biometric information of children in schools, etc.

Additionally, if a child refuses to take part in programs where biometric data are processed, or if a child refuses to have their biometric data processed, even if a parent gave their consent, then the relevant authority must ensure that reasonable alternative means are available by which the child may do, or be subject to, anything which the child would have been able to do, or be subject to, had the child's biometric information been processed.[57]

PFA also includes the definition of biometric information and of biometric recognition systems. In PFA, "biometric information" means information about a person's physical or behavioral characteristics or features which:

a. is capable of being used in order to establish or verify the identity of the person, and
b. is obtained or recorded with the intention that it be used for the purposes of a biometric recognition system.

The biometric information may, in particular, include:

a. information about the skin pattern and other physical characteristics or features of a person's fingers or palms,
b. information about the features of an iris or any other part of the eye, and
c. information about a person's voice or handwriting.[58]

The British legislator foresaw that in the catalogue of biometric data, new biometric characteristics (modalities) can appear in the future, so the phrase "in particular" is used (in order not to exclude other modalities). Even though PFA is a regulation which, in a comprehensive way, handles many aspects of new biometric technologies, one can have concerns with regard to some specific provisions.

In particular, PFA does not provide a closed catalogue of modalities which can be collected from children. The risk is that the relevant school bodies will collect data not specifically mentioned in the act, such as e.g., DNA data. The aforementioned list of modalities just gives examples, and the provision does not have the closed character. As a consequence, violations of privacy may result. Such a solution can also enable using other data collected from children in biometric systems. This paper shows that some biometric data can be more sensitive

---

57 See *PFA 2012*, Part 1 — Regulation of biometric data; Chapter 2 — Protection of biometric information of children in schools etc., point 26 (5)(6).
58 *PFA 2012*, Part 1 — Regulation of biometric data; Chapter 2 — Protection of biometric information of children in schools etc., p. 22.

than other. Such sensitive data are DNA, which contains the information about health[59].

It is worth mentioning that other sections of this Act regulate such aspects as: processing of data in surveillance systems, protection from inappropriate actions of law enforcement agencies, freedom of information, and data protection.

5 Legal regulations concerning the processing of biometric data in selected European countries

The regulations presented here show that some national legal frameworks do not fall behind the rapid developments in biometric technology.

The personal data protection regulation of Slovenia[60] contains detailed provisions concerning the processing of biometric data. In Article 6, point 21, biometric characteristics are defined as such physical, physiological, and behavioral characteristics which all individuals have, but whichare unique and permanent for each individual specifically, and which can be used to identify an individual, in particular by the use of fingerprints, recording of papillary ridges of the finger, iris scan, retinal scan, recording of facial characteristics, recording of an ear, DNA scan and characteristic gait.

The abovementioned provision points to biometric data. The regulations in Slovenia also indicate that biometric dataare sensitive data if they can be used to identify a person and meet the criteria mentioned in the regulation. According to Article 6, point 19, "[s]ensitive personal data - aredata on racial, national or ethnic origin, political, religious or philosophical beliefs, trade-union membership, health status, sexual life, the entry in or removal from criminal record or records of minor offenses that are kept on the basis of a statute that regulates minor offenses (hereinafter: minor offense records); biometric characteristics are also sensitive personal data if their use makes it possible to identify an individual in connection with any of the aforementioned circumstances." Moreover, this act contains the chapter on biometrics

---

59 D. Jaroszewska-Choraś, *Biometria – aspekty prawne*, Gdańsk 2016, *Supra* note 6, p. 112.
60 *Personal Data Protection Act (ZVOP-1)*, Official Gazette of the Republic of Slovenia, Nos. 86/2004, 113/2005 – ZInfP, 51/2007 – ZUstS-A and 67/2007. The Slovenian title is *Zakon o varstvu osebnih podatkov*. The Act was published on 05 August 2004. Then it was partially withdrawn, amended, and published again on 16 December 2005.

(Chapter 3), which is relevant for biometric data processing both in public[61] and private sectors.[62]

Slovenian regulations seem to stand out positively from most of other regulations. The Slovenian legislator noted a very important aspect, namely that there are two spheres where biometric technologies are used: the private sector and the public sector.

It has to be realized that biometrics can be used for public purposes, such as homeland security, and for private sector purposes (work time control, banks, sports arenas etc.). Therefore, it is really important (and most countries should work toward that end) to create legal guarantees and guidelines for processing biometric data in the private sector.

In point 78 of the Act, the purpose of biometric data processing is defined as follows: "the properties of an individual shall be determined or compared through the processing of biometric characteristics so as to identify him or confirm his identity (hereinafter: biometric measures) under the conditions provided by this Act."

The processing of biometric data in the public sector is regulated in Article 79, where: (1) Biometric measures in the public sector may only be provided for by statute if it is necessarily required for the security of people or property or to protect secret data and business secrets, and this purpose cannot be achieved by milder means. (2) Irrespective of the previous paragraph, biometric measures may be provided by statute where they involve compliance with obligations arising from binding international treaties or for identification of individuals crossing state borders.

This provision regulates the general rules for data protection, such as legitimacy and proportionality. The provision names special conditions for identification and verification. The processing of such data is allowed if there are legal grounds and the purpose in appropriately justified.

---

61 In point 22 of article 6, the concept of public sector was defined. Public sector are state bodies, bodies of self-governing local communities, holders of public powers, public agencies, public funds, public institutes, universities, independent institutions of higher education, and self-governing communities of nationalities.

62 In point 23 of article 6, the concept of private sector was defined. Private sector means legal or natural persons performing an activity in accordance with the statute regulating commercial companies or a commercial public service or craft, and persons of private law; public commercial institutes, public companies and commercial companies, irrespective of the share or influence held by the state, self-governing local communities or self-governing communities of nationalities.

Another aspect regulated in Slovenia is the application of biometrics in the private sector. Article 80 (1) states that the private sector may implement biometric measures only if they are necessarily required for the performance of activities, for the security of people or property, or to protect secret data or business secrets. Biometric measures may only be used on employees if they were informed in writing thereof in advance.

In this case, the provision defines the purpose for biometric data processing in a more abstract manner. In contrast e.g., to the Polish legislation, the statutory provisions in Slovenia allow for using biometrics at a workplace. The following condition has to be fulfilled: the employees have to be informed about the using of biometric data.

Therefore, it would be enough to state that biometric data processing is inevitable for some purposes or for the data controller. However, "if the implementation of specific biometric measures in the private sector is not regulated by statute, a data controller intending to implement biometric measures shall prior to introducing the measures be obliged to supply the National Supervisory Body with a description of the intended measures and the reasons for the introduction thereof."[63]

Then, the National Supervisory Body has to make a decision within two months[64] if the implementation of biometric technologies is in accordance with the act and provisions of Article 80. Additionally, the National Supervisory Body has to state if biometric systems, which control the work time of the employees from the public sector, are legal.

It is also worth mentioning the solutions from the Slovak act on personal data protection,[65] which regulates the processing of biometric data as sensitive data. This act states that biometric data shall mean personal data of the natural person based on which the person is clearly and unequivocally identifiable, e.g., fingerprint, palm print, analysis of DNA, DNA profile (section 4 (1) letter n).

Moreover, the Slovak act states (section 8(4)) that biometric data may only be processed under conditions stated in a special Act, provided that a) it expressly results for the controller from the Act; or b) the data subject gave a written consent to the processing.

---

63 See *Personal Data Protection Act (ZVOP-1)*, article 80 (2).
64 The two-month deadline can be extended by one month if the biometric technology at a workplace concerns at least 20 employees or if the representative of trade unions takes part in the administrative process.
65 Act No. 428/2002 Coll. On Protection of Personal Data, as amended by the Act No. 602/2003 Coll., Act No. 576/2004 Coll. and the Act No. 90/2005 Coll.

The Czech act for personal data protection from 4 April 2000,[66] in Article 4, letter b, also concerns biometrics. Similarly to the Slovak regulation, biometric data processing falls under the regulations for sensitive data processing.[67]

6 Conclusions

In this paper, we presented and discussed several legal acts and soft law documents that address the issue of biometry directly (fully or partly), but as we showed, those regulations are not fully coherent and do not cover all the aspects related to this issue. There is a new European Union law that will regulate this question, i.e., Regulation (EU) 2016/679 of the European Parliament and the Council of 27 April 2016 on the protection of natural persons with regard to the processing of personal data and on the free movement of such data, and repealing Directive 95/46/EC (General Data Protection Regulation). However, experts point to some issues which are not covered by this act and to the provisions that may lead to different interpretations, and consequently, it appears that some precision would still be needed at this level for biometric data to be well protected. Biometric technologies are developing at a fast pace and the range of human features used for biometric purposes will keep growing, so the regulations should be updated regularly in order to reflect those changes.

The analysis conducted in this paper shows that so far only few European countries have identified the need to adjust the regulations concerning personal data protection to the dynamically evolving biometric technologies.

The current existing national regulations should be evaluated positively. Firstly, those regulations contain much needed legal definitions of biometric data. Secondly, aspects of the usage of biometrics in private and public sectors are distinguished and regulated.[68] Thirdly, the purpose of and rules for biometric data processing are defined.

---

66 The Act for personal data protection number 101 of 04.04.2000, available at: https://www.uoou.cz/en/vismo/zobraz_dok.asp?id_ktg=1107&p1=1107 (last accessed 28.11.2017).
67 'Sensitive data' shall mean personal data revealing nationality, racial or ethnic origin, political attitudes, trade-union membership, religious and philosophical beliefs, conviction of a criminal act, health status and sexual life of the data subject, as well as any biometric or genetic data of the data subject'.
68 Such rules are included in the Slovenian personal data protection act.

Moreover, the procedures for audits and controls of biometric data processing by a special body are now in place. In particular, they concern biometric data processing in the private sector.

The provisions for personal data protection in Europe also show that, quite often, biometric data aspects are regulated within the frameworks and regulations concerning sensitive data. It means that biometric dataare interpreted as sensitive data.

Biometrics is deployed in many important operational spheres of countries and governments. It is common to use biometric technologies for homeland security, counterterrorism, fighting organized crime, as well as for the migration and asylum policies. However, using biometrics in such fields of the public sphere cannot infringe on the right to privacy or personal data protection. It is necessary to ensure clear and fair regulations for biometric systems deployment in accordance with the existing regulations. It needs to be emphasized that in duly justified cases the right to personal data protection and the right to privacy can be limited. Neither of these rights are of absolute nature. More often than not, the underlying reason for introducing such limitation is the need to ensure a broadly understood security for the entire society.

To conclude, danger lies in the fact that the necessary balance between the two values seems to be upset, and the "war on terrorism" becomes a justification for limiting personal data protection rights. Therefore, the legal principles and requirements should be fulfilled in ICT (Information and Communication Technologies) systems applied to security and counterterrorism.

Despite potential threats to fundamental human rights, and in spite of some ethical concerns, biometric technologies are becoming popular. Further developments in biometrics cannot be stopped, but the forthcoming regulations analyzed are needed in order to ensure that biometrics is regulated, controlled, and user-friendly.

Maciej Zejda

Applicable Law and Jurisdiction in Data Protection Law: Values behind the Source of Data Protection

The Internet enables cross-border data flows and thus becomes a key platform for commerce between buyers and sellers located in different countries. Understanding which set of rules governing data protection will apply to online data processing (particularly if the controller is established outside the European Union [EU]) is fundamental to the identification of that business's compliance obligations. This issue is of particular relevance to businesses that are based outside the EU, but conduct business in the EU, especially as the European data privacy reform takes one step forward to form a single digital union. Consequently, the long arm of the European data protection scheme may get even more far-reaching after coming into force of the General Data Protection Regulation (hereinafter: the GDPR). This paper will focus on the rules concerning jurisdiction and applicable law concretized notably in Directive 95/46/EC on the protection of individuals with regard to the processing of personal data and on the free movement of such data (hereinafter: Directive 95/46), i.e., rules which were in force until 25th of May 2018, and compare them with the changes introduced by the new legislation in this field, namely the GDPR, which applies from 25th May 2018. The article will specifically concentrate on the processing of personal data online, since in this case confusion as to the applicable law and competent jurisdiction arises most commonly as the activities of the controllers or processors are delocalized.

Public enforcement of the rules on personal data protection through Data Protection Authorities is still predominant in data protection enforcement and private claims before common courts are a rare practice.[1] A class action in Schrems v. Facebook case filed by 25,000 European citizens against Facebook before Austrian courts may be a milestone which shows that there is a role for

---

1   Communication from the Commission to the European Parliament, the Council, the European Economic and Social Committee and the Committee of the Regions, *Towards a European Horizontal Framework for Collective Redress* (COM(2013) 401 final).

private courts in data protection enforcement on a massive scale.[2] The involvement of courts in this kind of proceedings raises a question over jurisdiction and law applicable to the dispute on a regular basis. Consequently, providing an answer to the question of which set of rules applies may not only concern the compliance obligations of business owners but also be helpful for data subjects who feel harmed by the fact that business owners do not comply with the regulations governing data protection. The aim of this paper is thus not only to review jurisdictional and applicable law rules set in Directive 95/46 and compare them with the GDPR, but also to analyze the impact that the provisions governing applicable law and jurisdiction have on ensuring privacy protection and enhancing the productivity of the Internet as a forum for data processing and the relation between those two values in the light of recent judgments of the Court of Justice of the European Union (hereinafter: the CJEU).

1 Determination of applicable law pursuant to the EC Directive 95/46 on data protection

The rules on applicable law laid down by the data protection Directive 95/46 were described in its art. 4(1)(a), which provided for the application of national provisions of each Member State every time the processing is "carried out in the context of the activities of an establishment of the controller on the territory of the Member State." Furthermore, according to second part of art. 4(1)(a), if "the same controller is established on the territory of several Member States, it must take the necessary measures to ensure that each of these establishments complies with the obligations laid down by each national law applicable." It should be emphasized that Directive 95/46 did not have universal application, meaning that under its provisions only the law of one of the Member States and not law of a third country could apply.[3]

In order to establish which law applied according to art. 4(1)(a) to data processing, it was necessary to apply a two-stage test: whether the data controller had an establishment on the territory of a EU Member State, and if the controller processed personal data in the context of the activities of that establishment.[4] If those questions were answered in the positive, Directive 95/46 applied to such

---

2 Maximillian Schrems v Data Protection Commissioner, C-362/14.
3 M. Brkan, *Data Protection and European Private International Law*, Robert Schuman Centre for Advanced Studies Florence School of Regulation 2015/40, p. 31.
4 W. Kuan Hon, J. Hornle, C. Millard, *Data protection jurisdiction and cloud computing – when are cloud users and providers subject to EU data protection law? The cloud of*

personal data processing no matter where the processing took place. This provision gave rise to two important questions. Firstly, what is *an establishment*? And secondly, what does the phrase *in the context of the activities* mean?

It is clear from the wording of art. 4(1)(a) of Directive 95/46 that it applied to a processing even if the controller itself was not established in one of the Member States. The wording of art. 4(1)(a) of Directive 95/46 indicated the necessity of having an *establishment* rather *being established* in a certain jurisdiction. Pursuant to recital 19 of Directive 95/46, the establishment "implies the effective and real exercise of activity through stable arrangements" whereby the "the legal form of such an establishment, whether simply a branch or a subsidiary with a legal personality, is not the determining factor in this respect." The CJEU clarified in the *Google Spain* case that establishment requires at a minimum a staffed office with a degree of permanence and stability which exercises real and effective activity—even a minimal one—using its stable arrangements, while the legal form of such an establishment is not the determining factor.[5] Thus, it has been concluded that a subsidiary of the parent company satisfies the requirements of an establishment. Further on, in the *Weltimmo* case, the Court expressed the view that even the presence of just one representative, who acts as a point of contact between the controller and the data subjects and represents the controller in the administrative and judicial proceedings, could be considered sufficient to constitute an establishment.[6] Also, the CJEU clearly indicated that the nationality of the data subject had no impact on the aspect of the applicable law.[7] There was also a view presented in the doctrine that a branch office can be qualified as a controller for the purpose of art. 4(1)(a) as well since the lack of a separate legal entity of a branch was not a determining factor in establishing whether an entity can qualify as competent to decide on the purposes of data processing.[8]

The general rule developed by the CJEU was that art. 4(1)(a) of Directive 95/46 required the processing of personal data in question to be carried out not *by* the establishment concerned itself, but only *in the context of the activities* of

---

unknowing, International Review of Law, Computers & Technology 26, July–November 2012(2–3), p. 133.

5 Case C-131/12, Google Spain and Google, par. 48; Case C-230/14, Weltimmo and Nemzeti Adatvédelmi és Információszabadság Hatóság, par. 30–31.
6 Case C-230/14, Weltimmo and Nemzeti Adatvédelmi és Információszabadság Hatóság, par. 33.
7 *Ibidem*, par. 40.
8 L. Moerel, *Back to Basics: When Does EU Data Protection Law Apply?*, International Data Privacy Law, January 2011, p. 8.

the establishment.⁹ It has been raised by the CJEU as well that the processing is in the context of the activities of the establishment even if the establishment does not carry out or direct any processing itself, and its role is limited to being responsible for the relations with users of the search engine or the selling of advertisements in that jurisdiction. According to the judgment in the *Google Spain* case, the processing of data took place in the context of an establishment "when the operator of a search engine sets up in a Member State a branch or subsidiary which is intended to promote and sell advertising space offered by that engine and which orientates its activity towards the inhabitants of that Member State."[10] As a consequence, it has been held by the Court that the national law of the Member State of the subsidiary's establishment would still have applied, although there was no processing of data in this establishment and the controller had other establishment on the territory of the Union which processes data. This interpretation has been confronted with the exact wording of Recital 18 of Data Protection Directive 95/46, which explicitly stated that "processing carried out under the responsibility of a controller who is established in a Member State should be governed by the law of that State." In a scenario where a non-European controller had more than one establishment on the territory of the Union, but only one of them actually processesed personal data, the European subsidiary that processesed personal data could have been treated as a sole establishment within the meaning of art. 4(1)(a) of Directive 95/46. This proposition was in opposition to the reasoning of the Court presented in the *Google Spain* case. However, it has been noted in the literature that such an outcome would have been more adequate given the wording of Directive 95/46.[11]

The CJEU also stressed that it is essential to determine the existence of an "inextricable link" between the activities of an establishment in the Union and data processing by a non-European controller in order to assess that the processing is in the context of that establishment.[12] In this particular case, the CJEU decided that the sales generated by Google's local establishment in Spain were "inextricably linked to the profit made through the data processing activities - irrespective of where these actually took place - and that such 'inextricable' link was sufficient to trigger the applicability of the national law."[13] Further on,

---

9 Case C-131/12, Google Spain and Google, par. 52.
10 *Ibidem*, par. 60.
11 M. Brkan, *Data Protection...*, p. 34.
12 Case C-131/12, Google Spain and Google, par. 52.
13 Article 29 Data Protection Working Party, Update of Opinion 8/2010 on applicable law in light of the CJEU judgement in Google Spain, p. 4.

the CJEU concluded that "the activities relating to the advertising space constitute the means of rendering the search engine at issue economically profitable and that engine is, at the same time, the means enabling those activities to be performed."[14] It must be highlighted that the CJEU signaled that the "subsidiary which is intended to promote and sell advertisement space offered by the controller must orientate its activities towards the individuals of that Member State."[15] This kind of "orientating of activities" does not concern the directing of the activities of a controller or processor from one Member State to another, but rather the directing of activities to the Member State of the subsidiary establishment of the controller.[16]

Nevertheless, a wide interpretation of the phrase "context of the activities of an establishment" led to two kinds of consequences. Firstly, that Directive 95/46 applied even if no processing of personal data was carried out at the establishment, and secondly, that if more than one establishment was involved in the activities (taking into consideration that those activities could have had a secondary role in reference to the processing), the controller was subject to two or more different national implementations.

Consequently, art. 4(1)(a) abandoned the country of origin principle, according to which the controller must have complied only with the laws of the Member State where it is established, and allowed for the accumulation of applicable laws depending on the number of its establishments.[17] The application of two sets of laws may in some areas have been contradicting each other and provided for undesired results of such an interpretation of art. 4(1)(a). The broad interpretation of the concept of *context of the activities of an establishment* by the CJEU in the *Google Spain* case led to an even stronger fragmentation of applicable laws within the EU. The judgment in the *Google Spain* case sygnalised also a smooth shift from the territoriality principle to the effects principle, since

---

14 Case C-131/12, Google Spain and Google, para. 56 – this point made by the CJEU is a reflection of the opinion of Advocate General Jääskinen, who stated that the "processing of personal data takes place within the context of a controller's establishment if that establishment acts as the bridge for the referencing service to the advertising market of that Member State, even if the technical data processing operations are situated in other Member States or third countries." AG opinion, para. 67.
15 Case C-131/12, Google Spain and Google, par. 60.
16 M. Brkan, *Data Protection...*, p. 22.
17 L. Moerel, *Back to Basics...*, p. 5.

Member States were empowered to regulate activities which have not happened on their territory but which had effects within their territory.[18]

Besides the content of art. 4(1)(a), another source of rules on applicable law was contained in art. 4(1)(c) of Directive 95/46. This provision emphasized the long-arm approach of Directive 95/46, stipulating that a national data protection law applied also in the event that "the controller is not established on the territory of the Union and, for the purposes of processing personal data, makes use of equipment, automated or otherwise, situated on the territory of said Member State, unless such equipment is used only for the purposes of transit through the territory of the Union." In those circumstances, the controller must have designated a representative established in the territory of that Member State, in order to make it possible to initiate a legal action against the controller himself. It is of essence to emphasize that there was no requirement that the personal data processed have to relate to European individuals. Consequently, Directive 95/46 may have applied to the data subjects who did not have any connection with the Union except for the fact that their data were processed with the use of equipment situated on the territory of the Union. The *use of equipment* test was a variation on the physical presence test for jurisdiction that is commonly used as a basis for establishing jurisdiction.[19]

There was, however, a possibility of a loophole in art. 4(1)(c) due to the fact that the *equipment use* criterion could have been applied only if the controller was not established on the territory of the Union. As a result, when the controller was established within the territory of the Union but have not processed personal data in the context of that establishment's activities, then art. 4 (1)(a) did not apply. In such a scenario, art. 4 (1)(c) (the equipment ground) did not apply either, as the controller was established within the territory of the Union. This might mean that a controller may have been exempted from the application of EU data protection law if it had an establishment within the territory of the Union but did not process personal data in the context of that establishment's activities.[20] The Article 29 Working Party interpreted that provision and assumed

---

18 B. Van Alsenoy, M. Koekkeok, *"Internet and jurisdiction after Google Spain: the extraterritorial reach of the EU's" right to be forgotten"*, Working Paper No. 152 – March 2015, available at: https://ghum.kuleuven.be/ggs/publications/working_papers/2015/152vanalsenoykoekkoek. Last access: April 12, 2018.
19 O. Tene, C. Wolf, *Overextended: Jurisdiction and applicable law under the EU General Data Protection Regulation*, Future of Privacy Forum, January 2013, available at: https://fpf.org/wp-content/uploads/FINAL-Future-of-Privacy-Forum-White-Paper-on-Jurisdiction-and-Applicable-Law-January-20134.pdf. Last access: April 12, 2018.
20 W. Kuan Hon, J. Hornle, C. Millard, *Data Protection...*, p. 150.

that, in these circumstances, such an establishment was an *irrelevant establishment* which was of no importance in the context of the application of art. 4(1)(c).[21] However, given the reasoning in the *Google Spain* case, additional problems may have arisen since the activities of a European establishment may be somehow linked to the processing of data by a non-European controller. Nevertheless, the Article 29 Data Protection Working Party stated that provision 4(1)(c) of Directive 95/46 would apply where the controller had no establishment within the Union or the establishment was irrelevant.

From the perspective of jurisprudence, the definition of *equipment* was the most controversial aspect of this provision. According to academic writing, the equipment did not necessarily have to be something solid, tangible, or materially substantive.[22] Furthermore, the controller did not have to be the owner of the equipment.[23] It is, however, believed that the controller must have had some control over the equipment.[24] The Article 29 Data Protection Working Party established that the installation of a cookie file by a remote, non-European service provider would amount to making use of equipment in a Member State, leading to the application of that Member State's data protection law.[25] Consequently, it has been emphasized by the Article 29 Data Protection Working Party that Directive 95/46 was applicable to social networking sites, owned by a business which had no headquarters on the territory of the EU.[26] In such circumstances, the equipment criterion may led to the application of all Member States' data protection laws if e.g., the service provider was the controller and provided services to users across the Union. Furthermore, it was possible that Directive 95/46 would also apply when the processing had little or no connection with the Union, as the processing was undertaken by a non-European controller on non-European data subjects, but using equipment located within the Union's territory.[27] As a consequence, the equipment criterion had been repeatedly criticized as being misleading and not workable for controllers established outside the Union and running cloud businesses.[28] Moreover, the geographic overexpansion of the

---

21 Article 29 Data Protection Working Party, Opinion 8/2010 on applicable law, p. 19.
22 W. Kuan Hon, J. Hornle, C. Millard, *Data Protection...*, p. 138.
23 Article 29 Data Protection Working Party, pp. 20–21.
24 *Ibidem*, pp. 20–21.
25 *Ibidem*, p. 21.
26 Article 29 Data Protection Working Party, Opinion 5/2009 on online social networking, p. 5.
27 Article 29 Data Protection Working Party, Opinion 8/2010 on applicable law, p. 21.
28 W. Kuan Hon, J. Hornle, C. Millard, *Data Protection...*, p. 149.

scope of application of Directive 95/46 was said to result in unenforceability, as the decisions of supervisory authorities or court judgments rendered on the basis of the Directive could not have been legally exercised outside the borders of the Union.[29] It has been widely criticized that the application of the equipment rule led to a regulatory overreaching—"a situation in which rules are expressed so generally and non-discriminatingly that they apply to a large range of activities without having much of a realistic chance of being enforced."[30]

Directive 95/46 did not apply in principle if the equipment used for the purposes of processing personal data was used by a controller established outside the Union only for the purposes of transit through the territory of the Union. The reason for such an exclusion of the directive's application may have been that the mere transit of data through the territory of the Union does not pose a threat to European individuals.[31] An example of such actions may be the processing of data in telecommunication or postal services as long as service providers conduct a mere transit of data, rather than (as is nowadays usual) provide additional services, such as spam filtering.[32] In such circumstances, it is reasonable to assume that the data protection standard should have been relaxed.[33] However, this criterion for the exclusion of the applicability of Directive 95/46 was not harmonized uniformly throughout the Member States. In effect, the practical impact of this exclusion was hugely undermined. Some Member States excluded the application of Directive 95/46 only when transit took place through their own national territory, some referred only to "transit," and some, like France, have not implemented this exclusion at all.[34] Consequently, the transit criterion for exclusion led to many practical problems in determining when the application of Directive 95/46 is excluded.

Finally, it must be highlighted that pursuant to art. 4(1)(b), the national laws were applicable also when the controller was not established on the Member

---

29 O. Tene, C. Wolf, *Overextended: Jurisdiction…*
30 L. Bygrave, *Determining Applicable Law Pursuant to European Data Protection Legislation*, Computer Law & Security Report, 16, 2000, pp. 252–257; B. Maier, *How Has the Law Attempted to Tackle the Borderless Nature of the Internet?*, International Journal of Law & Information Technology, 18, 2010, p. 161.
31 L. Moerel, *The Long Arm of EU Data Protection Law: Does the Data Protection Directive Apply to Processing of Personal Data of EU citizens by Websites Worldwide?*, International Data Privacy Law, November 2010, p. 10.
32 Article 29 Data Protection Working Party, Opinion 8/2010 on applicable law, p. 23.
33 W. Kuan Hon, J. Hornle, C. Millard, *Data Protection…*, p. 149.
34 *Ibidem*, p. 149.

State's territory, but in a place where its national law applied by virtue of international public law. This provision inserted a derogation from the general principle embodied in art. 4(1)(a), under which the national law of the controller would apply if it had no relevant establishment within the territory of the EU. According to the Article 29 Data Protection Working Party, this provision referred to circumstances where "international public law or international agreements determine the law applicable in an embassy or a consulate, or the law applicable to a ship or airplane."[35] In those cases, the applicable national data protection law would be the one determined by international law.

Apart from the interpretation of provisions contained in Directive 95/46, there were various controversies regarding the relation between Regulation (EC) No 593/2008 of the European Parliament and of the Council of 17 June 2008 on the law applicable to contractual obligations (Rome I) and Regulation (EC) No 864/2007 of the European Parliament and of the Council of 11 July 2007 on the law applicable to noncontractual obligations (Rome II) and art. 4 of Directive 95/46. It may have been inferred from the view taken by the CJEU in *Google Spain* case that data protection lied outside the scope of Rome I and Rome II Regulations, and thus Directive 95/46 was treated as the sole source of rules on applicable law with respect to data protection. This opinion wass based upon the wording of Rome II Regulation, which by virtue of art. 1(g) excludes from its operation "non-contractual obligations arising out of violations of privacy." Consequently, it can be said that the CJEU has seen data protection as part of privacy and thus left it outside the application of Rome II Regulation.[36] On the other hand, it can be argued that there existed a *lex generalis–lex specialis* relation between those systems. This can be assumed on the strength of art. 23 and art. 27 from Rome I and Rome II Regulations, respectively, which expressly indicate that it is possible for other legal instruments to contain conflict of laws rules governing particular scope of matters.

If it is assumed that art. 4 of Directive 95/46 was *lex specialis* in relation to the Rome I and Rome II Regulations, it was necessary to assess whether national law which transposes art. 4 constituted an overriding mandatory provision in this jurisdiction and, consequently, whether it had an impact on freedom of choice provisions. A ruling of a German court located both legal instruments in the *lex generalis–lex specialis* relation.[37] Consequently, the rules on applicable laws

---

35 Article 29 Data Protection Working Party, Opinion 8/2010 on applicable law, p. 18.
36 M. Brkan, *Data Protection*..., pp. 27–28.
37 Case 8 B 60/12, Facebook Ireland Ltd. v Independent Data Protection Authority of Schleswig-Holstein, Germany.

contained in Directive 95/46 were classified by the Court as mandatory overriding provisions (in German law), which cannot be derogated and as such excluded the possibility to enter into an agreement on applicable data protection law.[38] The outcome of this decision did not necessarily mean that in every Member State data protection laws were given the status of mandatory overriding provisions. The ruling of the German court, however, indicated that controversies arising out of the relation between the Rome regime and Directive 95/46 were not only of academic importance. Thus, the impact of the agreements on applicable law may have been divergent due to the status of data protection regulations in certain jurisdiction, assuming that the *lex generalis–lex specialis* relation prevailed.

2 Jurisdiction under Directive 95/46

The Directive did not include jurisdictional rules which resemble provisions on the scope of the applicability of the national laws of the Member States. art. 28(6) of Directive 95/46 did, however, refer to the territorial scope of competence enjoyed by supervisory authorities that may have applied and enforced the applicable law. Nevertheless, this provision referred merely to the administrative path of litigation and is thus outside the scope of this paper.[39] Directive 95/46 contained a rule which allowed any data subject to appeal against supervisory authority's decisions through courts. Such proceedings did not constitute a civil or commercial matter within the meaning of Regulation 1215/12 of the European Parliament and of the Council of 12 December 2012 on jurisdiction and the recognition and enforcement of judgments in civil and commercial matters (hereinafter: Regulation 1215/12) since the supervisory authority acted as a public authority. Thus, Regulation 1215/12 was not the source which indicated jurisdiction in the case of a data protection litigation against decisions of supervisory authorities. Consequently, this aspect was also not covered by this article. However, by virtue of art. 23 of Directive 95/46, it was possible for the data subject to initiate claim against the controller for damages in case of a loss suffered due to an unlawful processing operation or of any act incompatible with the national provisions adopted pursuant to Directive 95/46. This provision introduced a civil path of litigation, which, as regards jurisdiction, was governed by Regulation 1215/12.

---

38 For more information, see: Case 8 B 60/12, Facebook Ireland Ltd. v Independent Data Protection Authority of Schleswig-Holstein, Germany; also see: M. Brkan, *Data Protection*…, p. 29.
39 Article 29 Data Protection Working Party, Opinion 8/2010 on applicable law, p. 10.

In the cases of civil litigations regulated by Regulation 1215/12, consideration must be given to several issues: the general rule, contractual jurisdiction, consumer jurisdiction, contractual prorogation of jurisdiction (with emphasis on its permissibility in relation to consumers), and jurisdiction in the case of proceedings related to a tort.

The general principle of Regulation 1215/12 is located in art. 4(1). The *actor sequitur forum rei* rule is a standard test for assessing jurisdiction if the parties have not concluded a specific agreement on the choice of the jurisdiction. It is important to note that if the defendant is domiciled outside the Union, Regulation 1215/12 will in principle not be applicable and a European data subject who wanted to exercise its rights could have only relied on the rules of private international law of its own Member State.[40] Another aspect which has to be considered is the concept of an *establishment* used in Directive 95/46 and the concept of *domicile* in Regulation 1215/12. It is believed by some authors that the legal unification of both these notions would be helpful to facilitate determining the jurisdiction.[41]

Further on, consideration must be given to contractual jurisdiction—i.e., a situation when data subject concludes a contract with the controller or processor. According to art. 7(1)(a) of Regulation 1215/12, a controller domiciled in a Member State may be sued in another Member State in matters related to a contract, in courts competent for the place of performance of the obligation in question. It has been highlighted by commentators that the general contractual jurisdiction indicates the jurisdictions for claims arising out of infringements of data protection, as they are encompassed by the notion of *matters related to a contract*.[42] The place of the performance of an obligation can be understood twofold, depending on the character of the contractual relationship. In the case of the sale of goods, the place of the performance of the obligation is in the Member State where, under the contract, the goods were delivered or should have been delivered.[43] In the case when services are the subject of the contractual performance, the place of the performance of the obligation is in the Member State where, under the contract, the services were provided or should have been provided.[44] In principle, this division is clear and the conclusion of a contract online has no impact on the characteristic features of the agreement itself. However,

---

40 M. Brkan, *Data Protection*..., p. 12.
41 *Ibidem*, p. 13.
42 *Ibidem*, p. 17.
43 Art. 7 (1)(a)(b), Regulation 1215/12.
44 Art. 7 (1)(a)(b), Regulation 1215/12.

there is a number of questions regarding the qualification of certain agreements as contracts for sale or contracts for services, since in the Internet environment the majority of the market is focused on contracts involving incorporeal, digitized products, software delivered online being the best example. In such circumstances, it is difficult to say whether those kinds of transactions are sales or services contracts.[45] Furthermore, the definition of the place of performance of the obligation in online transactions is also obscure, although in the case of contracts of sale the place of delivery is usually inserted in the contract itself. However, there is a number of scenarios when the problem with determining the place of performance arises, e.g., when the parties do not indicate the place of delivery in their contract for the sale of digitized goods or the contract is qualified as a service agreement. In such circumstances, there are a number of places where those electronic transactions are processed, e.g., the place of dispatch and receipt, the place where the seller has a specified personal connecting factor, and the place where the recipient (i.e., the buyer) has a specified personal connecting.[46] There is also a position which supports the view that in the case of service agreements offered online the decisive factor is whether it is the activity or the result of that activity, i.e., uploading or downloading.[47] Nevertheless, the majority of authors state that it is the place of the recipient of a service which shall determine the jurisdiction.[48]

The application of rules on contractual jurisdictions becomes even more complex if the data subject is also a consumer. Regulation 1215/12 sets a rule upon which a consumer may choose whether to commence proceedings against the controller with which he or she contracted before the courts of the Member State in which the controller is domiciled or before the courts for the place where the

---

45 There is a strong argument presented by commentators of the CISG that "software" shall be qualified as a goods for the purpose of the convention, although depending on the provisions of every single contract. Consequently, it can be argued that from the perspective of the CISG such a contract shall be qualified as sale. However, it must be highlighted that in a scenario when the transaction is not governed by the CISG (and this is the case in most popular online transaction, since parties most commonly decide to exclude the application of this instrument), the character of the contract will be determined on the basis of the national law.

46 F. F. Wang, *Obstacles and Solutions to Internet Jurisdiction: A Comparative Analysis of the EU and US Laws*, Journal of International Commercial Law and Technology, 3, 2008, p. 237.

47 P. Mankowski, in: U. Magnus, P. Mankowski, *Brussels I Regulation*, Munich 2012, p. 189.

48 F. F. Wang, *Obstacles and Solutions…*, p. 237.

consumer is domiciled.[49] However, in order to enable the consumer to sue before courts in its jurisdiction, it must be established that the contract was concluded for the purposes which are outside the consumer's trade or profession and simultaneously the service provider was pursuing commercial or professional activities in the Member State of the consumer's domicile or, by any means, directing such activities to that Member State or to several States including that Member State.[50] In light of the CJEU's case law, the consumer may not use the contracted service or goods for professional purposes at all, as even the slightest non-marginal use of the services or goods in trade may trigger a *regular* contractual jurisdiction.[51] Given the last requirement, it can be argued that these days, when the majority of internet users smoothly switch from the private use to professional use of certain online services, such as Facebook or Gmail, it would be difficult to establish the consumer's contractual jurisdiction. This is an interesting situation, since the data subject can only be a natural person, so it is highly possible that in many situations it may act as a consumer. However, the determination of the jurisdiction regarding the data protection disputes, which is dependent on whether the data subject, who is always a natural person, contracted for the purposes outside its professional scheme, seemed as not a far reaching protection of data subjects, given the character of many online services and doubts over the qualification of certain agreements as services or sale contracts. A more accurate solution would probably require the imposition of a rule implying special jurisdiction for disputes connected to data protection, which would always vest in the country of the data subject origin.[52]

Further on, the necessity of proving that the commercial or professional activities of the controller are directed to the consumer's origin Member State is also challenging. The CJEU expressed its view on whether a website operator directs its activities to a particular Member State in the *Pammer/Alpenhof* case.[53] This case-law indicated that the business entity needs to manifest its intention to establish commercial relations with consumers from one or more other Member States, including that of the consumer's domicile. As a result, the CJEU, in the *Pammer/Alpenhof* case, established a test which requires taking into account all evidence surrounding the website and the trader's commercial activities in

---

49 Art. 18, Regulation 1215/12.
50 Art. 17(1)(c), Regulation 1215/12.
51 Case C-464/01, Johann Gruber v Bay Wa AG, par. 39.
52 M. Brkan, *Data Protection…*, p. 24.
53 Case C-585/08, Pammer and Hotel Alpenhof, par. 93.

order to assess whether the trader was targeting the consumer's domicile—those evidences are inter alia:

- the international nature of the activity,
- use of a language or a currency other than those used in the trader's place of establishment
- mention of telephone numbers with international dialing code,
- marketing focused on the consumer's domicile such as keyword advertising
- use of a top-level domain other than that of the Member State in which the trader is established,
- the description of itineraries from one or more other Member States to the place where the service is provided,
- mention of an international clientele composed of customers domiciled in various Member States, in particular by presentation of accounts written by such customers.[54]

There are concerns regarding the legal meaning of the language or currency used on the website. It is generally believed that they do not constitute relevant factors for the purpose of determining whether an activity is directed to one or more other Member States. If, on the other hand, the website permits consumers to use a different language or a different currency, the language and/or currency can be taken into consideration and constitute evidence from which it may be concluded that the trader's activity is directed to other Member States.[55] Additionally, the CJEU expressed its opinion that it is not the consumer who is responsible for providing a proof of an intention on the part of the trader to develop activity on a certain scale with those other Member States.[56] In the *Emrek* case, it has been concluded as well that "a causal link between the means of directing an activity through an internet site and the actual conclusion of a contract is not necessary."[57]

Finally, a prorogation agreement, which deprives the consumer of his or her right to sue the controller before the consumer's national courts, could have very rarely be enforced. Regulation 1215/12 states that "a prorogation agreement may be concluded with a consumer only if it is entered into after the dispute has arisen, or allows the consumer to bring proceedings in other courts, or if it is entered into by the consumer and the controller both of whom at the time of

---

54 *Ibidem*, par. 83.
55 *Ibidem*, par. 84.
56 *Ibidem*, par 83.
57 Case C-218/12, Lokman Emrek v Vlado Sabranovic, par. 32.

conclusion of the contract domiciled or habitually resident in the same Member State, and the prorogation agreement must confer jurisdiction on the courts of that Member State."[58]

Regulation 1215/12 establishes a rule that in matters relating to tort, delict, or quasi-delict the harmed person may sue in the courts for the place where the harmful event occurred or may occur.[59] According to the test formulated in the *eDate Advertising* case, the place where the harmful event occurred or may occur can mean one of the following three locations: the jurisdiction of the courts of the establishment of the controller, the courts of the center of interests of the data subject, or, according to the *mosaic theory*, for damage caused in the territory of a particular Member State, the courts of each Member State in the territory of which content placed online is or has been accessible.[60] The result of the application of those rules to tortious data protection infringements have led to parallel proceedings, as data subjects could have been harmed in different sets of jurisdictions by the same act of the same controller. Such an outcome was highly unfavorable as it would allow for the rendering of contradictory judgments regarding the same act of the controller and thus led to severe obstacles concerning enforcement of such decisions.

3 The EU General Data Protection Regulation (the GDPR)—revision of the rules on applicable law

The EU GDPR does not contain a conflict-of-laws provision similar to art. 4 of Directive 95/46. The reason why the GDPR lacks such a provision is because it itself unifies the national laws on the processing of data. Consequently, commentators have observed that after the entry into force of the GDPR, the question of which law applies shall no longer in principle be relevant.[61] This notion is not 100% correct as the GDPR will not basically replace all relevant national laws but both systems will have to coexist and interact.[62] An example of a situation where the GDPR builds on a national law is provided by art. 6(1) of

---

58 Art. 19, Regulation 1215/12.
59 Art. 7(2), Regulation 1215/12.
60 Case C-509/09, eDate Advertising and Others, par. 52.
61 M. Brkan, *Data Protection…*, p. 35.
62 P. Hustinx, *EU Data Protection Law: The Review of Directive 95/46/EC and the Proposed General Data Protection Regulation*, available at: http://www.statewatch.org/news/2014/sep/eu-2014-09-edps-data-protection-article.pdf. Last accessed: April 12, 2018.

the GDPR.[63] The GDPR also requires, in some instances, that the national law should lay specific provisions in certain areas, such as in the case of art. 6(2) of the GDPR. Thus, there is a certainty that data protection laws will differ between Member States. One single set of applicable rules will not exist and thus the assessment of the relation between the Union law and national law will "require careful study and fine tuning, both at EU and at national level."[64] Consequently, it has been raised in the doctrine that the coming into force of the GDPR will not eliminate once and for all conflicts of laws within the Member States.[65] One instance where such conflicts may arise refers to a scenario where the Member States, despite the GDPR, maintain in force various provisions on issues not contained in the GDPR.[66] Another problem is related to the possibility to make a contractual choice of applicable of law for data protection agreements and the enforcement of such agreements concluded before the GDPR comes into force. Probably, such prorogation agreements would be forbidden under the GDPR, since it is impossible for the parties to a contract to derogate from the application of a regulation.

Although the GDPR does not regulate the aspect of the applicable law, it contains a provision regarding its territorial scope of application, which, similarly to art. 3 of Directive 46/95, distinguishes between situations where the controller is established in the EU or otherwise. By virtue of art. 3(1), the GDPR "applies to the processing of personal data in the context of the activities of an establishment of a controller or a processor in the Union." The meaning and application of the concepts of *establishment* and *context of activities* are also not clarified adequately by the GDPR. The GDPR broadened the scope of its application by introducing a rule according to which it applies to the processing of personal data not only in the context of the activities of an establishment of a controller but also of an establishment of a processor in the Union. It also introduced a concept of *main establishment* to deal with intra-Union conflicts where there are establishments of controllers or processors in multiple Member States. According to art. 4(16), the main establishment' means, in respect of

---

63 According to Article 6(1) of the GDPR, the processing of personal data shall be lawful if and to the extent that such processing is (c) necessary for compliance with a legal obligation to which the controller is subject, or (e) necessary for the performance of a task carried out in the public interest or in the exercise of official authority vested in the controller.
64 P. Hustinx, *EU Data Protection*..., p. 36.
65 M. Brkan, *Data Protection*..., p. 35.
66 P. Hustinx, *EU Data Protection*..., p. 30.

the controller, "the place of its central administration in the Union, unless the decisions on the purposes and means of the processing of personal data are taken in another establishment of the controller in the Union and the latter establishment has the power to have such decisions implemented, in which case the establishment having taken such decisions is to be considered to be the main establishment. Correspondingly, as regards the processor, its main establishment is the place of its central administration in the Union, or, if the processor has no central administration in the Union, the establishment of the processor in the Union where the main processing activities in the context of the activities of an establishment of the processor take place to the extent that the processor is subject to specific obligations under this Regulation."

Additionally, the preamble of the GDPR explains that the main establishment of a controller in the Union should be determined according to objective criteria and should imply the effective and real exercise of management activities determining the main decisions as to the purposes and means of processing through stable arrangements. Further on, it states that a "criterion should not depend on whether the processing of personal data is carried out at that location. The presence and use of technical means and technologies for processing personal data or processing activities do not, in themselves, constitute a main establishment and are therefore not determining criteria for a main establishment. The main establishment of the processor should be the place of its central administration in the Union or, if it has no central administration in the Union, the place where the main processing activities take place in the Union."[67] If the processing is carried out by a group of undertakings, the main establishment of the controlling undertaking should be considered to be the main establishment of the group of undertakings, except where the purposes and means of processing are determined by another undertaking.

As a consequence of this division, the GDPR introduced a concept of a lead competent supervisory authority. In the circumstances where both the data controller and data processor are involved in data processing, the main establishment is that of the data controller and the competent lead supervisory authority should be the supervisory authority of the Member State where the controller has its main establishment. However, this does not mean that the supervisory authority of the processor should not be considered to be the supervisory authority concerned as it should participate in the cooperation procedure stipulated by the GDPR. It can be thus assumed that the aim of introducing the

---

67 Recital 36, GDPR.

concept of a *main establishment* is not to solve problems regarding the understanding of the concept of *an establishment* but to resolve possible conflicts of competences between supervisory authorities in cases of data processing in several Member States. The wording of the GDPR remains unchanged compared to the wording of Directive 95/46 regarding the concepts of *establishment* and *context of activities*.[68] Thus, the reasoning of the CJEU in the case of *Google Spain* will be applicable also after the entry into force of the GDPR, since the adoption of the concept of *main establishment* is purely for the purpose of solving conflicts of competences between local authorities in the administrative path of litigation.[69] This is an unfortunate outcome, since European establishments of controllers and processors situated outside the territory of the Union will have to comply with the data protection laws of several Member States and not just with the law of the Member State where the main establishment is located.

Article 3(2) of the GDPR applies to "the processing of personal data by a controller not established in the EU, where the processing activities are related to offering of goods or services to such data subjects in the Union irrespective of whether a payment by the data subject for the goods or services is required." Consequently, the GDPR replaces the concept of the equipment criterion with a test similar to the targeting/directing test encountered previously in relation to the assessment of consumer jurisdiction under Regulation 1215/12. This innovation establishes a total shift from the country of origin regulation to the effects principle and the passive nationality principle as regards applicable law in a data protection scheme. The practical outcome of such a change is that all the companies running their businesses online based outside the territory of the EU and not having an establishment on the territory of the Union will have to comply with the European data protection legislation when they offer goods or services online to European data subjects. This new rule seems to be built upon the reasoning of the CJEU in the *Google Spain* case, where it stipulated that the national law of the Member State of an establishment of the controller which is not processing any personal data would still apply if it orientates its activities toward the individuals of that Member State.[70]

There are three main problems related to the test mentioned in art. 3(2)(a) of the GDPR. First of all, it is difficult to assess when the controller's activities are related to the offering of goods or services. Is only the occasional offering

---

68   Recital 22, GDPR.
69   M. Brkan, *Data Protection…*, p. 32.
70   Case C-131/12, Google Spain and Google, par. 60.

of goods sufficient to establish that the controller relates its activities in a way which triggers the application of the GDPR?[71] This aspect may cause uncertainty, especially in the case of electronic commerce, as webpages are accessible from any country in the world. In such circumstances, it is difficult to assess when the services/products are offered to the data subjects in the Union.

The preamble of the GDPR is once again of assistance, this time as regards the issue of whether the offering of services/goods is related to a particular Member State. According to its provision, "in order to determine whether such a controller or processor is offering goods or services to data subjects who are in the Union, it should be ascertained whether it is apparent that the controller or processor envisages offering services to data subjects in one or more Member States in the Union. It has been noted that the mere accessibility of the controller's, processor's or an intermediary's website in the Union, of an email address or of other contact details, or the use of a language generally used in the third country where the controller is established, is insufficient to ascertain such intention, factors such as the use of a language or a currency generally used in one or more Member States with the possibility of ordering goods and services in that other language, or the mentioning of customers or users who are in the Union, may make it apparent that the controller envisages offering goods or services to data subjects in the Union."[72]

It can be noted that the assessment of whether certain services or goods are offered to individuals in the Union resembles the test developed by the CJEU in connection with the interpretation of Regulation 1215/12, which provides for jurisdictions in a consumer's domicile in cases involving consumer contracts when a party "by any means, directs such activities to that Member State or to several countries including Member State."[73] Firstly, it must be emphasized that the GDPR does not require the offering of the goods or services to take place in respect of the Member State where the data subject is domiciled. It is thus sufficient to trigger the application of the GDPR if the services or goods are offered to such data subjects in the whole territory of the Union. Secondly, it must be stressed that the wording of art. 3(2)(a) of the GDPR differs from the wording of art. 15(1) of Regulation 1215/12 as it uses a phrase "related to" rather than "aimed at." It can be noticed that the phrase "related to" has a broader sense than the phrase "aimed at" and may cause the application of the GDPR even if potentially

---

71 W. Kuan Hon, J. Hornle, C. Millard, *Data Protection...*, p. 153.
72 Recital 23, GDPR.
73 Art. 17(1), Regulation 1215/12.

no risk to privacy exists. As a consequence, it is impossible to apply directly the test created in reference to Regulation 1215/15 consequently the GDPR will apply more often than provisions on consumer jurisdiction contained in Regulation 1215/15.[74] Some authors comment that the GDPR would be more workable if the words "related to" in art. 3(2) were replaced with the words "aimed at" and thus clearly provided for the purposeful targeting test explained by the CJEU in the Pammer/Alpenhof case.[75]

On the other hand, counter-productive effects could arise if it was intended for the phrases "related to" and "aimed at" to have a similar scope of application. In such scenario tests developed by the CJEU in respect of determining jurisdiction in a consumer's domicile in cases involving consumer contracts would act as a yardstick for assessing the application of the GDPR. However, rules developed in the Pammer/Alpenhof case and other cases would not harmonize the aspects of jurisdiction and applicable law since the GDPR contains a set of rules on jurisdiction separate from those imposed by Regulation 1215/12, which are commented upon in details later on. Pursuant to the jurisdictional rules regarding the civil litigation path set in art. 79(2) of the GDPR, proceedings against a controller or a processor may be brought in any case before the courts of the Member State where the data subject has his or her habitual residence, unless the controller or processor is a public authority of a Member State acting in the exercise of its public powers. Data subjects are thus always able to sue controllers or processors before courts located in their jurisdiction, unlike consumers, who are limited by the directing/targeting test.

As a result, the application of the tests developed under Pammer/Alpenhof case and following cases to the phrase "related to" contained in art. 3(2) of the GDPR may lead in certain circumstances to situations whereby the jurisdiction would vest in every case in the data subject's domicile but the applicable law would not be of the same Member State, as it would be assessed that the activities of the controller or processor are not related to the Member State in which the data subject is domiciled. As a consequence, better data protection of individuals can be afforded if the phrase "related to" is treated as having a broader meaning than the phrase "aimed at" contained in Regulation 1215/12 since that way

---

74 P. Schwartz, *EU Privacy and the Cloud: Consent and Jurisdiction Under the Proposed Regulation*, Privacy & Security Law Report, 12, p. 718, available at: https://www.paulhastings.com/docs/default-source/PDFs/eu_privacy_and_the_cloud__consent_and_jurisdiction_under_the_proposed_regulation.pdf. Last access: April 12, 2018.

75 O. Tene, C. Wolf, *Overextended: Jurisdiction...*

parallelism between jurisdiction and applicable law in the case of data protection disputes can be achieved.

Secondly, there is a necessity to assess which party the burden of proof lies with; it is essential to establish who would be required to prove that the controller relates or does not relate its activities to a particular Member State while offering its goods or services. This time, we could possibly follow the rules created by the CJEU in respect of determining jurisdictions in a consumer's domicile in cases involving consumer contracts as there is no counter-indication for taking such steps arising out of the wording of the GDPR in this respect. It can also be noted that the position of data subjects and consumers is in principle similar since both are perceived as the weaker party. As a result, the burden of proof will possibly lie with the controllers or processors.[76] Consequently, it is probably the controller or processor who would be required to prove that it was not its intention to develop an activity of a certain scale within the territory of the Member State where the data subject is domiciled.

The GDPR applies also to the processing of personal data by a non-European controller or processor if the processing is related merely to the monitoring of the data subject's behavior as far as their behavior takes place within the Union. This criterion links to the passive personality principle, pursuant to which jurisdiction can be exercised over acts wherever they are carried out if they cause harm to nationals of the country claiming jurisdiction.[77] As it is stated in the preamble of the GDPR, "in order to determine whether a processing activity can be considered to monitor the behaviour of data subjects, it should be ascertained whether natural persons are tracked on the internet including potential subsequent use of personal data processing techniques which consist of profiling a natural person, particularly in order to take decisions concerning her or him or for analysing or predicting her or his personal preferences, behaviours and attitudes."[78] There are views expressed in the doctrine that the concept of *monitoring* would be better suited to achieve the aims of the GDPR if it was understood more narrowly and was restricted only to situations where the observation of an individual is linked to privacy risks.[79] In many situations, a mere observation of a data subject, which may include the initial stages of the collection and analysis of information, e.g., for the sake of rejecting unsafe browsers from logging in to cloud services, should

---

76 Case C-585/08, Pammer and Hotel Alpenhof, par. 83.
77 D. J. B. Svantesson, *Extraterritoriality in the Context of Data Privacy Regulation*, Masaryk University Journal of Law and Technology 7(1), p. 93.
78 Recital 24, GDPR.
79 P. Schwartz, *EU Privacy and the Cloud…*

be placed outside the concept of monitoring as there is no privacy risk involved for an identified person during such observations. The broad understanding of the term *monitoring*, which links it to the term *profiling* included in the GDPR, suggests that any observation of a data subjects' behavior creates a threat to an EU data subject's privacy although in practice it is not true.[80] It must be noted that similarly to Directive 95/46 the GDPR applies also to the processing of personal data by a controller not established in the Union, but in a place where Member State law applies by virtue of public international law.

In summary, the new scheme of rules on the scope of the application of the European data protection law requires the companies located outside Europe, with a customer base in the EU, to be mindful of the potential *long arm* of the GDPR more than in respect of Directive 46/95. The wording of art. 3(2) threatens to generate a conflict with other privacy regimes. Under the rule of art. 3(2), companies with little or no geographical connection to the Union are expected to comply with EU law. Consequently, a business operating online must be aware of the necessity to comply with obligations arising from a distant jurisdiction that may provide different rights and responsibilities than the jurisdiction of the business owner. This risk is even more serious as businesses and individuals increasingly use cloud computing services which store data on remote servers that could be located in any country in the world. However, problems with an extraterritorial application of European data protection scheme already existed under the *use of equipment* test in art. 4(1)(c) of Directive 95/46. Under the GDPR, the application of European law is more clarified and better suited to protect European individuals although it does not create one single set of rules regarding data protection. Geographic expansion of the application of the GDPR may also lead to the unenforceability of the obligations set in the GDPR.

Furthermore, the GDPR does not exclude its application where data are only in transit, through the jurisdiction of an EU Member State. Such an exemption was guaranteed in the Directive's rules for jurisdiction over a controller who only uses equipment situated in EU for the sake of the transit of data. The omission of such a provision may have some impact on cloud computing services.[81] This is all the more unfortunate since the deletion of the equipment criterion in the GDPR would in principle mean that the Union law does not apply when non-European individuals' data are processed by a controller with no establishment within the

---

80 P. Schwartz, *Information Privacy in the Cloud*, University of Pennsylvania Law Review, 161, p. 1652.
81 *Ibidem*, p. 1652.

territory of the Union but which uses equipment located within the territory of the Union. There is a high possibility, though, that the transit-through exclusion would be read-in by the CJEU.

4 Jurisdictional rules contained in the GDPR

According to art. 78 (3) of the GDPR, "proceedings against a supervisory authority shall be brought before the courts of the Member State where the supervisory authority is established." This kind of proceedings, regulated similarly in Directive 95/46, fall outside the sphere of civil and commercial matters as defined by Regulation 1215/12 as they concern administrative decisions of supervisory authorities. In these circumstances, the defendant—a local supervisory authority—acts as a public authority and it is widely accepted that those kind of disputes are outside the scope of the application of Regulation 1215/12.

The GDPR, however, contains provisions specifically designed to equip data subjects with remedies against infringements of data protection rules on the part of controllers or processors and corresponding jurisdictional rules which may be helpful for data subjects in order to exercise those remedies. The jurisdictional rules regarding the civil litigation path are set in art. 79(2) of the GDPR, which literally states that "proceedings against a controller or a processor shall be brought before the courts of the Member State where the controller or processor has an establishment. Alternatively, such proceedings may be brought before the courts of the Member State where the data subject has his or her habitual residence, unless the controller or processor is a public authority of a Member State acting in the exercise of its public powers." Additionally, the preamble of the GDPR provides that "the plaintiff should have the choice to bring the action before the courts of the Member States where the controller or processor has an establishment or where the data subject resides, unless the controller is a public authority of a Member State acting in the exercise of its public powers."[82] In these circumstances, the subject of the dispute falls within the sphere of *civil and commercial matters*, and, consequently, it is essential to assess the relation between those jurisdictional rules and other provisions of Regulation 1215/2012.

First of all it shall be underlined that personal jurisdiction of data subjects is no longer dependent on the type of contract the data subject entered with the controller or processor in the case of contractual jurisdiction as required by the general rules of Regulation 1215/12. Another aspect is that of whether

---

82 Recital 145, GDPR.

personal jurisdiction of the data subject requires the existence of the *targeting* of the controller's activities toward the Member State of the domicile of the data subject. At first glance it seems that there is no such requirement in jurisdictional rules provided by the GDPR. Consequently its basic rules on jurisdiction shall apply irrespective of *targeting* requirement. There are, however, comments suggesting that lack of this requirement may undermine the harmonization of rules on jurisdiction and applicable law.[83]

Unfortunately, the jurisdictional rules set in the GDPR do not clarify whether it is admissible to enter into a jurisdictional agreement in respect of disputes concerning data protection. Other concerns are related to the application of jurisdictional rules contained in the GDPR in contrast to the clauses on exclusive jurisdiction contained in Regulation 1215/12. Some authors uphold that a solution may involve the separation of the jurisdiction for data protection infringements from the exclusive jurisdiction provided by Regulation 1215/12.[84] Such an interpretation would possibly render forum selection clauses unenforceable when it comes to disputes between data subjects and controllers or processors.

5 Conclusions

The shift in the attitude toward the conflict-of-laws rules and jurisdictional rules indicates that the Union gives the highest priority to the data protection of its citizens. Information about individuals represents two values: the economic value of these data as seen from the perspective of business enterprises and their value in respect of the right to privacy of every natural person. Currently, those values are sometimes locked in a conflict due to expansive and anti-data protection policies of businesses located outside the territory of the Union. However, both of those values, which are embodied in the data protection scheme, can grow as a result of the extraterritorial application of the GDPR. First of all, every EU individual can rest assured that their right to privacy is effectively protected when they undertake actions online. Furthermore, under the GDPR, the data subject is equipped in more efficient tools to seek damages for data protection infringements as it is allowed to sue every controller or processor before their own national court under the national law nearly in every case of a data protection infringement. This outcome resembles the approach of the Union in respect of the consumer protection but is even more far-reaching. Some authors

---

83 M. Brkan, *Data Protection*…, p. 23.
84 *Ibidem*.

underline the dichotomy of data protection "as a rights oriented regulation and data protection as an economic regulation."[85] It is clear from the structure of jurisdictional and applicable law rules contained in the GDPR that the general purpose or rationale of data protection is ensuring the informational privacy of the individual citizen. Some authors criticize such jurisdictional approach as putting obstacles in a way of non-European businesses, thus leading to anti-competitive results which prevent the digital economy from growing.[86] This, however, does not have to be the case as the need for safe and secure Internet and the growth of the digital economy do not necessarily have to be at odds. First of all, the enhanced data protection scheme may find reflection in increased self-awareness of individuals who undertake activities online. One possible outcome of such a process is the creation of a society which is less afraid of online transactions in general and specifically of those with businesses located outside the EU as individuals are aware that the EU protection covers them no matter where the business enterprise they deal with is established. Consequently, the inevitability of the application of the protection afforded by the GDPR may apparently encourage people to use online transactions with enterprises located outside the EU but which undertake activities related to offering their goods or services on the territory of the specific Member State. Additionally, the ability to sue before the national courts in any case whereby the data subject's rights to privacy are infringed puts an end to all discussions regarding the interpretation of whether online transactions are mainly focused on the delivery of goods or performance of services and whether the characteristic performance takes place in delocalized online environment. Consideration must be also given to the influence online services (especially social services) may have on individuals and their decision-making. Such services are e.g., able to filter contents displayed to users by monitoring user's behavior. This new regulation may possibly help the online services market grow even faster and bigger as such services have become decreasingly credible in recent history when it comes to data protection policies.

Critics of the extraterritorial reach of the GDPR point out that it is not realistic to expect every business owner located outside EU to abide data protection rules laid down by the GDPR.[87] Firstly, the scope of the application of the European data protection scheme covers cases which concern processing personal data of European individuals. Secondly, it should be emphasized that the Union claims

---

85 P. Blume, *It is Time for Tomorrow. EU Data Protection Reform and the Internet*, Journal of Internet Law, 2, 2015, p. 6.
86 O. Tene, C. Wolf, *Overextended: Jurisdiction...*
87 L. Bygrave, *Determining Applicable...*

the right to regulate Internet activities of controllers and processors that are related in some way to the territory of the Union. Consequently, the notion that the far-reaching arm of the GDPR is excessive is disputable, as its application is always justified by the fact that the processing must concern individuals who live in the Union. It follows from art. 3 of the GDPR that the controllers or processors without an establishment in the Union must at least undertake activities in relation to offering goods on the territory of the Union or monitor the behavior of data subjects. Given the high number of operations on data subjects, such a link is strong enough to justify the application of the GDPR, and there is nothing wrong about the fact that the GDPR introduces a test which covers a broader scope of circumstances in comparison to the one used for establishing the consumer jurisdiction. Thirdly, it must be noted that the unclear concept of the equipment criterion used under art. 4 of the Directive 95/46 also led to the universal application of European data protection law. The requirement to comply with the law of every Member State aggravated the chaos regarding the various possible jurisdictions in respect of data protection disputes, made controllers' obligations much more complex, and undermined the effective protection of the data subject's rights compared to the scheme introduced by the GDPR. The directly binding GDPR brings greater harmonization and consistency of the Union law although it does not introduce a single applicable law. Under Directive 95/46, controllers were in practice obliged to abide by the national laws on data protection of respective Member States. After the entry into force of the GDPR, not much will change in this respect as the relation between the Union law and the national laws of respective Member States will also have to be analyzed in order to establish the relevant provisions binding controllers and processors. What will change is that jurisdictional chaos in reference to disputes related to data protection infringements will come to an end, and thus, controllers or processors will have to be aware of the fact they can be sued in the data subject's jurisdiction irrespective of the type of the source of infringement or character of data subjects' activities. The enhanced data protection by virtue of the extraterritorial application of the GDPR and the jurisdiction in civil path litigations vesting always in the domicile of the data subjects reflect the idea that the current European policy treats data protection as one of the most valuable rights but also notices that sensible protection of this information, in an era when data processing informs the market valuation of biggest businesses, is essential for allowing the online-services market to grow in a better-balanced manner. The only remaining problem with the growing extraterritorial scope of the application of the European data protection scheme is the ability to enforce this new law in respect of controllers or processors located outside EU. However, there is a possibility that the fear of adverse publicity which may affect an online service which does not obey European data protection rules may act as an incentive to comply with the data protection obligation, since damage to a company's reputation can ultimately cause it lot of harm in the marketplace.[88] Online service providers are aware of the significance of good publicity when reaching the EU market, which consists of over 500 million data subjects. As a result, it is possible that the long arm of the European data protection scheme may deter overseas companies from engaging in activities that might result in violating these rules.[89]

In conclusion, although the GDPR is not faultless, its approach toward jurisdiction and scope of application reinforces the rights of individuals as it ensures better enforcement of data protection rules as well as enhances the internal market dimension, additionally covering the global dimension of data protection compared to the results achieved under Directive 46/95.

---

88 D. J. B. Svantesson, *A Jurisprudential Justification for Extraterritoriality in (Private) International Law*, 13 Santa Clara Journal of International Law 517, 2015, p. 553.

89 Article 29 Data Protection Working Group, *Working Document on Determining the International Application of EU Data Protection Law to Personal Data Processing on the Internet by Non-E.U. Based Web Sites 15*, No. 56, 2002.

Richard Warner and Robert H. Sloan

Defending Our Data: The Need for Information We Do Not Have

Data breaches occur at the rate of over two a day.[1] The aggregate social cost is high. One recent study puts the average cost per business of a breach at $4 million.[2] Such estimates are controversial,[3] but it is clear that breaches impose significant losses on society. Security experts have long explained how to defend better.[4] So why does society tolerate a significant loss that it has the means to avoid?

---

1 Identity Theft Resource Center, Data Breach Reports, http://www.idtheftcenter.org/images/breach/DataBreachReports_2016.pdf, last access: 26 April 2018. The ITRC uses a narrow definition of a breach: a data breach is "an incident in which an individual name plus a Social Security number, driver's license number, medical record or financial record (credit/debit cards included) is potentially put at risk because of exposure." Unauthorized access to computers and networks can be "potentially put at risk because of exposure" a great deal of other sorts of sensitive information, so data breaches would be even more common on the correspondingly broader understanding of breach. Whatever the exact breach rate, there are enough breaches to impose significant costs on society.
2 *2016 Ponemon Cost of Data Breach Study: Global Analysis* (2016), http://www-03.ibm.com/security/data-breach/, last access: 26 April 2018. That $4 million is Ponemon's estimate of *data breach* costs as defined in the study, and is up from their estimates in previous years. Their 2015 study of cybercrime costs defines those costs more broadly and estimates them at $7.7 million per business annually. *2015 Ponemon Cost of Cyber Crime Study: Global Analysis* (2015), http://www.ponemon.org/blog/2015-cost-of-cyber-crime-united-states, last access: 26 April 2018.
3 M. Korolov, $154 or 58 cents – what's the real cost of a breached data record? CSO online (2015), http://www.csoonline.com/article/2931839/data-breach/154-or-58-cents-whats-the-real-cost-of-a-breached-data-record.html, last access: 26 April 2018.
4 There are numerous undergraduate and graduate textbooks on computer security discussing how best to defend. See, e.g., R. J. Anderson, *Security Engineering: A Guide to Building Dependable Distributed Systems*, 2nd ed. 2008; M. Goodrich & R. Tamassia, *Introduction to Computer Security* 2010; C. Kaufman, R. Perlman & M. Speciner, *Network Security: Private Communication in a Public World*, 2nd ed. 2002; C. Pfleeger, S. Pfleeger, J. Margulies, *Security in Computing*, 5th ed. 2015;

Some may object that society does *not* tolerate breaches. After all, laws—current and proposed—impose requirements aimed at improving information security. As the lawyer Thomas Smedinghoff notes, there are information security laws that "obligate companies to establish and maintain 'reasonable' or 'appropriate' security measures, controls, safeguards, or procedures."[5] However, Smedinghoff also notes that most of the laws "simply obligate companies to establish and maintain 'reasonable' or 'appropriate' security measures, controls, safeguards, or procedures, but give no further direction or guidance."[6] We contend that the consequence is that the laws fail to provide an adequate incentive to improve information security. The solution is to provide better guidance about what counts as reasonable security measures.

That solution may seem singularly unappealing since it requires having information that is currently unavailable about the magnitude of losses and the probability of their occurrence. Data breach notification laws may seem to offer an attractive alternative. They impose reporting requirements on businesses that suffer a data breach. Businesses can incur considerable costs in complying with those requirements, and, in response, they have increased online security. We argue that it is unlikely that the increase is actually an improvement and conclude that there is no alternative to finding some way to provide the currently unavailable information. The need for the information creates possible privacy concerns that we do not pursue here.

1 Technical background

An essential preliminary is a brief review of technological facts relevant to data breaches. The key point concerns vulnerabilities. A vulnerability is a property of a program, computer, or network that hackers can exploit to gain unauthorized access. Vulnerabilities come in three types: software, human, and network. We focus on networks, but first briefly review the other two types.

W. Stallings & L. Brown, *Computer Security: Principles and Practice*, 3rd ed. 2014. The SANS institute publishes a fairly short list of critical security controls, and argues that simply adopting the top five or so would vastly improve the information security posture of most organizations. See, e.g., SANS Institute, The CIS Critical Security Controls for Effective Cyber Defense, http://www.sans.org/critical-security-controls/, last access: 26 April 2018.

5 T. Smedinghoff, *Defining the Legal Standard for Information Security: What Does "Reasonable" Security Really Mean?*, Securing Privacy in the Internet Age, Chander, Gelman, & Radin eds., 2008, pp. 19–40.

6 *Ibidem.*

1.1 Software vulnerabilities

Think of a vulnerability as an unlocked door. The hacker finds it and walks in. Software programs currently contain an unacceptable number of unlocked doors. That is not inevitable. Software engineers know how to minimize (though alas not how to totally eliminate) vulnerabilities.[7] How to write individual computer programs well, and the basics of software engineering are fairly well-settled subjects.[8] The basics of high-quality code construction and software engineering generally form a significant fraction of the core (required) portion of the model computer science bachelor's degree curriculum jointly published by the two main professional societies for computer science in 2013[9] (and also did so in earlier model curricula[10]). Years of studies confirm the common wisdom among

---

7 Software is different from other engineered products in that sufficiently complex software inevitably has some programming flaws. As far back as the 1980s, a panel convened to study the issues with software for President Regan's Strategic Defense Initiative noted, "Simply because of its inevitable large size, the software capable of performing the battle management task for strategic defense will contain errors. *All systems of useful complexity contain software errors.*" Strategic Def. Initiative Org., Dep't of Def., 19980819-140. Eastport Study Group: Sumer Study 1985. A Report to the Director, Strategic Initiative Organization 14 (1985), http://dodreports.com/ada351613, last access: 26 April 2018. (emphasis added). Recently, Capers Jones noted that one goal of software engineering best practices is to increase the percentage of bugs removed prior to delivery from 85 percent to something that "approach[es] 99 percent," (*not* that it approaches 100%). JONES, *supra* note 114, at xxvi. In contrast, design flaws are not inevitable in, for example, refrigerators, batteries, and bridges even when they exhibit considerable complexity. Software alone combines complexity and inevitable flaws. Thus, no matter how much one invests in development procedures designed to reduce programming flaws, flaws—and perhaps vulnerabilities—will remain.
8 However, the choice of *which* software engineering methodology is the best one for managing various sorts of projects is contentious. In particular, there is debate about the relative merits of a traditional methodology called the Waterfall Model with its origins in the late 1960s versus various other methodologies, such as Spiral or Agile. *See, e.g.,* D. Parnas, *A Rational Design Process: How and Why to Fake it*, 3, http://www.cs.tufts.edu/~nr/cs257/archive/david-parnas/fake-it.pdf, last access: 26 April 2018. (criticizing the Waterfall Model); K. Beck et al., *Manifesto for Agile Software Development*, 2001, http://agilemanifesto.org/, last access: 26 April 2018. (outlining the Agile Model).
9 The Joint Task Force on Computing Curricula, Association for Computing Machinery (ACM), IEEE Computer Society, Computer Science Curricula 2013: Curriculum Guidelines for Undergraduate Degree Programs in Computer Science (2013), https://www.acm.org/education/CS2013-final-report.pdf last access: 26 April 2018.
10 E. Roberts et al., Computing Curricula 2001: Computer Science, 2001.

experts in software development that proper attention to software development leads to lower defect rates.[11]

So why is software so full of vulnerabilities? In large part because reducing vulnerabilities requires a longer and more costly development process. Consumers have been unwilling to pay for the added value of security through slightly higher retail prices, and companies dependent on consumer sales do not offer what consumers do not want. "Businesses are profit-making ventures, so they make decisions based on both short- and long-term profitability,"[12] and the "market often rewards first-to-sell and lowest cost rather than extra time and cost in development,"[13] The typical profit-maximizing strategy is to keep costs down and be the first to offer a particular type of software, even if it is imperfect in a variety of ways, including having vulnerabilities.[14]

We have discussed software vulnerabilities and a possible remedy in detail elsewhere.[15]

---

11 *See generally* Anthony Hall, *Seven Myths of Formal Methods*, 7 IEEE Software 11, pp. 11–19 (Sept. 1990) (discussing Praxis studies and the CASE project). *See also* I. J. Hayes, *Applying Formal Specification to Software Development in Industry*, SE-11 IEEE Transactions on Software Engineering 169, Feb. 1985 pp. 175–176 (discussing the usefulness of software engineering techniques in some particular projects); A. MacCormack et al., *Trade-offs between productivity and quality in selecting software development practices*, 20 IEEE Software 78, pp. 81–84 (Sept.–Oct. 2003) (comparing various software engineering techniques).
12 *Ibidem.*
13 E. Spafford, *Remembrances of Things Pest*, 53 Comm. ACM, 2010, pp. 35–36.
14 C. Shapiro & H. R. Varian, Information Rules: A Strategic Guide to the Network Economy, 1999, pp. 50–51. The economics and information security community has developed Shapiro and Varian's initial insights. Much of this work has been reported in the annual Workshop on the Economics of Information Security since 2002. For information on the workshops from 2002 to 2010, see http://weis2010.econinfosec.org/index.html, last access: 26 April 2018. For a good general survey, see R. Anderson & T. Moore, *Information Security: Where Computer Science,* Economics and Psychology Meet, 367 Phil. Transactions Royal Soc'y, 2009, pp. 2717, 2721–2722.
15 R. Sloan, R. Warner, *Unauthorized Access: The Crisis in Online Privacy and Information Security* (2013); Richard Warner & Robert H. Sloan, *Vulnerable Software: Product-Risk Norms and the Problem of Unauthorized Access*, Univ. Ill. J. Technol. Law Policy 2010, p. 101.

1.2 Human vulnerabilities

The main human vulnerability hackers exploit is the human propensity to trust. Vampire movies are a good analogy. In classic vampire movies, vampires cannot enter a house unless invited in, so the audience cringes when some innocent, ignorant person asks the obvious-to-the-audience vampire to cross the threshold. Far too many invite hackers to cross the threshold of their computers and networks. Phishing is a good example. Phishing is the use of an electronic communication that masquerades as being from someone trustworthy in order to gain unauthorized access to information. For example, in a case study entitled, "Examining how a China-based threat actor stole vast amounts of PII," Mandiant notes that

> Phishing attacks continue to be a theme year after year, and this case is no different. It began with a threat actor successfully enticing a user to follow a malicious link in a phishing email. The link downloaded a backdoor, providing the threat actor access to the victim's environment. Once the threat actor obtained a foothold, the reconnaissance activity was primarily centered on the identification of databases with the greatest volume of PII.[16]

Phishing is by no means the only way hackers masquerade themselves to exploit people's trust. Other examples include various other forms of social engineering[17] and Trojan horses.[18]

The way to reduce human vulnerabilities is hardly a mystery. It is a matter of adequate education and training.

1.3 Network vulnerabilities

Software is involved in running a network, so some network vulnerabilities are software vulnerabilities, and human beings use networks, so human vulnerabilities are also common. But not all network vulnerabilities are software or human ones. From now on, we will use "network vulnerabilities" for the

---

16 Mandiant, *M-Trends 2016 FireEye* 17, https://www.fireeye.com/current-threats/annual-threat-report/mtrends.html, last access: 26 April 2018.
17 Social engineering is pretending to be someone else in order to gain access to a computer or network, or, more generally, to obtain any confidential information. Skip tracers (professionals specializing in locating people) have practiced social engineering for years, and so have debt collectors, bounty hunters, private investigators, and journalists. Phishing does this via email or malicious websites.
18 A Trojan Horse is malicious program masquerading as a safe and useful one.

non-software, non-human vulnerabilities in networks. They are the ones whose remediation requires information that is not currently available.

To characterize network vulnerabilities, we need a sketch of how network security works. It works a lot like security at the United Center, the sports arena where the Bulls play basketball and the Blackhawks play hockey. If you were in charge of security there, you would find out where the doors are, lock the ones you do not need and post guards at the rest to check credentials (tickets, press passes, etc.). Nothing is perfect, so you also would put guards inside to monitor behavior. Computer and network security is the same. You lock doors (shut down access points[19]), post credential-checking guards (verify authorization[20]) and deploy behavior-monitoring guards (ranging from home computer antivirus programs to multimillion-dollar systems defending corporate networks[21]).

It is difficult to implement these practices without creating vulnerabilities. In a large organization, both the routers and internal structure of the network can be quite complex, and the more complex the network, the more likely a misjudgement that creates a vulnerability. Even a highly skilled network administrator can find it extraordinarily difficult to predict what software will do when it is embedded in a complex network. In addition, hackers "are well aware of network … security mechanisms, and are developing increasingly sophisticated and effective methods for subverting them."[22] Thus, in a complex network it is common to find at least a few vulnerabilities.

Network administrators know—or should know—how to reduce network vulnerabilities.[23] Wyndham Hotels' security provides an illuminating example—of what *not* to do. Wyndham is a reasonably large organization, and it has valuable consumer data, such as credit card numbers. Wyndham's security was egregiously bad. Its security failures were at the center of *FTC v. Wyndham Worldwide Corp.*[24] Among the important weaknesses, Wyndham hotels evidently had no firewalls

---

19 Examples include vulnerability detection, promptly applying security patches, using reasonably up-to-date operating systems, and various uses of encryption.
20 Examples include passwords, more complex multi-factor identification, access control, firewalls, and both black and white listing.
21 Examples include intrusion detection and protection systems, some forms of malware detection, and various forms of monitoring traffic.
22 A. Gupta et al., *An Empirical Study of Malware Evolution*, in Communication Systems and Networks Workshops, COMSNETS 2009, pp. 1–10.
23 *Ibidem*, p. 4.
24 FTC v. Wyndham Worldwide Corp., 799 F. 3d 236, D. C. 2015.

at all and stored credit card numbers in the clear (i.e., unencrypted).[25] There is simply no question that adequate security requires an organization the size of Wyndham to, among other things, have a hardware firewall, store sensitive data in encrypted form, and patch regularly. Failures in any one of these areas constitute wholly inadequate security.[26]

Wyndham's failures illustrate specific ways for security to be inadequate. At a higher level of abstraction, we distinguish two ways for security to be inadequate: inadequate defense of others, and inadequate self-defense. We begin with the defense of others. A business may, as Wyndham certainly did, fail to adequately protect consumers from losses consumers suffer as a result of the business's data breach. The problem is that Wyndham is no outlier. Businesses *typically* fail to adequately protect consumers. The reason is that profit motive-driven businesses ignore customer and third party losses unless those losses also impose significant losses on the business.[27] Organizations have

> insufficient incentives to invest in strong data security and accountable privacy practices because, in essence, they didn't have to. Consider that lost or "stolen" customer or employee data often does not deprive an organization of its continued availability or use, as would loss or theft of physical property. Further, the (negative) consequences of poor security and misused data fall mainly if not entirely upon individual victims, often at a later date.[28]

"Reasonableness standard" laws respond to this situation by attempting to create a legal incentive to reduce consumer's harm from unauthorized access. We contend that a lack of relevant information makes the incentive seriously inadequate.

Our argument begins, seemingly paradoxically, not with a focus on consumer losses, but with a focus on losses to *businesses*. There are two reasons. First,

---

25 Other significant lapses were that Wyndham had absolutely no restrictions on where people could log in from (i.e., no restrictions on any specific IP addresses) and had various passwords that were unchanged from the original factory setting.
26 This is not to say that adequate network security is a fully settled subject. One might ask such questions as: "Does a home user or a very small business need a firewall," "What type of firewall should a medium to large organization use," and "Will any firewall stop a determined nation-state attacker?"
27 B. Dean et al., *Sorry Consumers, Companies Have Little Incentive to Invest in Better Cybersecurity Quartz*, http://qz.com/356274/cybersecurity-breaches-hurt-consumers-companies-not-so-much/ (accessed June 26, 2016).
28 A. Cavoukian, *A Discussion Paper on Privacy Externalities*, Security Breach Notification and the Role of Independent Oversight, 2009, pp. 5–6, https://www.ipc.on.ca/images/Resources/privacy_externalities.pdf, last access: 26 April 2018.

that is where the failure to adequately protect consumers begins. The less able businesses are to defend their networks against unauthorized access, the greater the potential for harm to both the business *and* consumers. Second, the lack of information problem arises for businesses' attempts to avoid purely business losses, and, to the extent it has been studied, it has been most extensively studied in that context.

The perhaps surprising fact is that businesses' *self-defense* is typically inadequate. As one commentator summed up the situation, "[t]he bad guys basically go where they want to go and do what they want to do, and they're not being stopped. Maybe for every one organization that's effectively stopping attacks, there are 100 that are being breached."[29] What is striking is that adequate defense clearly maximizes profits. More precisely, the profit maximizing approach is to pursue the following *risk management goal*: choose the most effective defense meeting the condition that the defense cost is not greater than expected business losses thereby avoided (over some appropriate short- or long-term time period).[30] We will call this the *business* risk management goal to distinguish it from the *consumer* risk management goal we will introduce later, where the goal is to reduce *consumer* losses.

One reason businesses fall short of a good approximation to business risk management goal is that corporate culture has struggled to incorporate that goal in its business planning.[31] This is evidently changing. At least,

> In the wake of increased cyber attacks, business leaders have grown to understand that both the financial and reputational impact an information security breach has on an organization can be devastating. As a result, board members have become more educated on information security matters, which has led to increased involvement in the cyber risk reduction process. Of board members surveyed in our study, 89% indicated that they are "very involved" in making cyber risk decisions.[32]

---

29 G. Hulme, *Security Spending Continues to Run a Step Behind the Threats CSO Online*, 2013, http://www.csoonline.com/article/2134074/strategic-planning-erm/security-spending-continues-to-run-a-step-behind-the-threats.html, last access: 26 April 2018.
30 Implementing this strategy faces significant problems in practice. It can be difficult to evaluate the effectiveness of various security measures. Relevant costs and benefits may not be quantifiable, and those that are may only be roughly and approximately so. In addition, costs and benefits may be quite difficult to predict.
31 *Underinvesting in Cybersecurity: How Do You Know How Much Security Is Enough?*, 2014, http://www.symantec.com/connect/blogs/underinvesting-cybersecurity-how-do-you-know-how-much-security-enough, last access: 26 April 2018.
32 *How Boards of Directors Really Feel About Cyber Security Reports*, Bay Dynamics 2, http://baydynamics.com/resources/how-boards-of-directors-really-feel-about-cyber-security-reports/, last access: 26 April 2018.

However, it is still not "common for IT and security executives to report information about the cost of the organization's cyber security program, identification of which security controls are working, and ways in which the company's cyber risk program can be improved."[33] Without accurate information about costs and benefits, there is simply no way for a business to adequately manage risk.[34]

We assume that corporate culture will eventually embrace the business risk management goal. That will not, however, eliminate the fundamental problem: namely, the lack of information necessary for adequate risk assessment. A recent World Economic Forum report paints an accurate, if disturbing, picture of the lack of relevant data.

> There are numerous cyber threats plaguing global organizations. Global data is expanding at exponential rates in terms of volume, velocity, variety and complexity. Commercial and personal data are increasingly migrating to global, interconnected technology platforms. The systems that depend upon this data increasingly manage key infrastructure. As access to data and systems increases via the rapidly evolving, interconnected digital ecosystem, the scale and types of risks from cyber threats expands proportionately.
>
> Unknowns concerning the scale and impact of cyber threats, as well as relative levels of vulnerability, threatens paralysis. Lacking accepted benchmarks, large organizations struggle to structure cyber resilience decisions and investments. Organizations lack common measures to quantify cyber threats, curtailing the ability to make clear strategic decisions concerning optimal access and investment levels.
>
> Due to this state of uncertainty, a pervasive concern over growing cyber risks curtails technical and economic development on a global scale. Lacking proper guidance, businesses are increasingly delaying the adoption of technological innovations due to inadequate understandings of required countermeasures. A tragedy of the commons scenario is emerging surrounding proliferating digital access in an unstable ecosystem, which lacks concerted controls and safeguards. A vicious circle results: uncertainty regarding proper levels of preparedness leads to forestalled investments in safeguards as interconnection expands exponentially.[35]

---

33 *Ibidem*, p. 5.

34 C. Veltsos, *What CISOs Need to Tell The Board About Cyber Risk Dark Reading*, 2016, http://www.darkreading.com/operations/what-cisos-need-to-tell-the-board-about-cyber-risk/a/d-id/1325923, last access: 26 April 2018. This is not to deny the point D. Thaw astutely notes: even without guidance about what counts as reasonable, requiring businesses to base security decisions on a reasonable assessment of risk can improve security. David Thaw, *The Efficacy of Cybersecurity Regulation*, 30 Ga. State Univ. Law Rev. 2015, p. 287.

35 World Economic Forum, Partnering for Cyber Resilience Towards the Quantification of Cyber Threats World Economic Forum 9, 2016, http://www3.weforum.org/docs/WEFUSA_QuantificationofCyberThreats_Report2015.pdf. Others make the same

The report identifies two sources of uncertainty. The first is that the magnitude of the losses is not sufficiently well known: there are "[u]nknowns concerning the scale and impact of cyber threats." The second is that the probability of a loss is not sufficiently well known: there are "[u]nknowns concerning relative levels of vulnerability." This puts a significant roadblock in the way of pursuing the business risk management goal. That requires reasonably reliable estimates of the expected losses avoided, and that requires reasonably reliable estimates of the magnitude of the relevant losses and of the probabilities of their occurrence.

Lack of data is not a problem just for the pursuit of the business risk management goal. The same roadblock also stands in the way of reducing loses to consumers from data breaches, and it plays a key role in explaining the current ineffectiveness of "reasonableness standard" laws in creating adequate incentives for businesses to improve their ability to defend consumers from losses. We turn to those laws in the next section.

2 Reasonableness standards

Reasonable standards for network defense have a compelling theoretical rationale. We explain that rationale and conclude that, ideally, the law should provide appropriate standards for what counts as a reasonable assessment of the risk of loss from a data breach. We then turn to the question of why, as Smedinghoff notes, most of the laws "simply obligate companies to establish and maintain 'reasonable' or 'appropriate' security measures, controls, safeguards, or procedures, but give no further direction or guidance."[36] We argue that the problem is that risk assessment requires reliable information about both the magnitude of the loss and the probability of its occurrence, and sufficient information of that sort is not currently available. We conclude that, at the moment, the "reasonableness standard" approach fails to provide an adequate incentive for business to protect consumers from harm from unauthorized access.

---

points: "It has also long been known that we simply do not have good statistics on online crime, attacks and vulnerabilities. Companies are hesitant to discuss their weaknesses with competitors even though a coordinated view of attacks could allow faster mitigation to everyone's benefit. In the USA, this problem has been tackled by information-sharing associations, security-breach disclosure laws and vulnerability markets." Ross Anderson et al., Security Economics and European Policy 3, 2008, http://www.cl.cam.ac.uk/~rja14/Papers/enisa-short.pdf.

36 T. Smedinghoff, *Defining the Legal...*, p. 5.

2.1 The rationale

How does one ensure that businesses adequately defend against consumer losses from unauthorized access? To begin with, we note that approximating the *business* risk management goal is far from irrelevant. Business losses can impose costs on consumers. They do so to the extent that businesses recoup their losses through higher prices or through cost-savings that reduce the quality of products and services. Thus, adequate business self-defense can reduce costs to consumers. As we noted earlier, we assume that businesses will eventually embrace the goal of adequate business risk management. Assume, for the sake of argument, that they in fact do so. Indeed, assume they do not just approximate the goal, but realize it perfectly. Are there *still* losses to consumers that businesses should take steps to prevent by further improving their defenses?

The question divides into two. First, are there significant losses to consumers from unauthorized access that remain even after perfect business risk management? And second, if so, should businesses also take steps to reduce those losses? We assume the answer to the first question is "Yes." There is remarkably little available data, but the studies that do exist suggest that the losses are significant.[37] Given the losses, we assume that one should pursue the following *consumer* risk management goal: choose the most effective defense meeting the condition that the defense investment equals the expected *consumer* losses thereby avoided

---

[37] In 2014 the aggregate loss in the United States from identity theft was around $100,000,000. E. Harrell, *Victims of Identity Theft 2014*, 2015, http://www.bjs.gov/index.cfm?ty=pbdetail&iid=5408, last access: 26 April 2018. Earlier United States estimates of the cost of identity theft alone are also in the billions. For a summary of relevant studies, see Fred H. Cate, Information Security Breaches and the Threat to Consumers, Ctr. for Info. Pol'y Leadership at Hunton & Williams 6, Sept. 2005, http://www.fredhcate.com/Publications/Information_Security_Breaches.pdf (reporting 10.1 million victims of identity theft in 2003 and a total losses to consumers of over 50 billion). Identity theft estimates ignore non-identity theft losses from, for example, ransomware, denial of services attacks, botnets engaged in fraud and other illegal activities, and viruses. A United Kingdom government study with a broader focus estimates the yearly cost of data breaches to be £21bn to businesses, £2.2bn to government and £3.1bn to citizens. Detica, The Cost of Cybercrime 2 (Feb. 2011), http://www.cabinetoffice.gov.uk/sites/default/files/resources/the-cost-of-cyber-crime-full-report.pdf. For a follow-up study, see R. Anderson et al., *Measuring the Cost of Cybercrime*, in *Eleventh Workshop on Economics of Information Security*, 2012, weis2012.econinfosec.org/papers/Anderson_WEIS2012.pdf.

(over some appropriate time period).[38] The question is, *who* should defend? Businesses or consumers?

There is a strong argument that businesses should bear a considerable part of the defensive burden. That argument is the rationale for "reasonable standard" laws. A good way to present the argument is by an analogy with landlords and tenants. The "landlords" are the various kinds of businesses that store consumer data online.[39] Call them collectively *data holders*. "Tenants" divide into the data that resides with the data holder and the consumer subjects of that data. What makes the analogy apt is that unauthorized access to the data can harm the subjects. The argument is that just as landlords can be liable for harm to tenants for harm from unauthorized access to the landlords' buildings, so should data holders be liable for harm caused to consumers by unauthorized access to the data they store. To see the argument, consider the landlord/tenant case, *Kline v. 1500 Massachusetts Avenue Apartment Corporation*.[40] Kline was assaulted in the common areas of the apartment building in which she lived. She sued for negligence alleging that the building owner unreasonably failed to provide adequate security. The court agreed:

> The landlord is no insurer of his tenants' safety, but he certainly is no bystander. And where, as here, the landlord has notice of repeated criminal assaults and robberies, has notice that these crimes occurred in the portion of the premises exclusively within his control, has every reason to expect like crimes to happen again, and has the exclusive power to take preventive action, it does not seem unfair to place upon the landlord a duty to take those steps which are within his power to minimize the predictable risk to his tenants.
>
> …
>
> As between tenant and landlord, the landlord is the only one in the position to take the necessary acts of protection required. He is not an insurer, but he is obligated to minimize the risk to his tenants. Not only as between landlord and tenant is the landlord best

---

38 There are two important qualifications. One is that the costs and benefits may be controversial, and may not all be quantifiable. The other is that in some cases, deciding by the cost/benefit comparisons inherent in risk management may be blocked by moral commitments. See S. Cho & R. Warner, *Comparison Excluding Commitments: Incomm ensurability, Adjudication, and the Unnoticed Example of Trade Disputes*, South. Calif. Law Rev. 2017. L. Tribe, *Policy Science: Analysis or Ideology?*, Philos. Public Aff. 1972, p. 66. Privacy concerns may be a case in point.
39 Businesses range from resource- and expertise-rich corporations to mom-and-pop retailers. There is a pressing question of how small and medium sized businesses are to meet the risk management goals we suggest here.
40 Kline v. 1500 Massachusetts Ave. Apartment Corp., F.2d 477 (1970).

equipped to guard against the predictable risk of intruders, but even as between landlord and the police power of government, the landlord is in the best position to take the necessary protective measures. Municipal police cannot patrol the entryways and the hallways, the garages and the basements of private multiple unit apartment dwellings. They are neither equipped, manned, nor empowered to do so. In the area of the predictable risk which materialized in this case, only the landlord could have taken measures which might have prevented the injuries suffered by appellant.[41]

The court holds that the landlord was required to take reasonable steps to defend tenants in common areas from harm from unauthorized access to those areas. Advances in technology have resulted in a new type of "landlord"—data holders. Like traditional landlords, they are typically in the best position to take steps to prevent the harm to data subjects that may follow a data breach. So why not require data holders to take reasonable steps to prevent harm to the data subjects?

We find this rationale compelling and conclude that the law should require data holders to sufficiently closely approximate the consumer risk management goal. This approach runs squarely into a lack of data problem very similar to the problem that plagues attempts to realize the business risk management goal.

2.2 The lack of data problem and its consequences

Successful risk assessment requires reasonably reliable estimates of the magnitude of the relevant losses and of the probabilities of their occurrence. For consumer risk management, the relevant magnitudes and probabilities are the magnitudes and probabilities of *consumer* losses. The reasons are essentially the same as they are for business risk management. Neither the magnitude of the losses nor the probabilities of those losses are sufficiently well known. The problem is particularly acute in the case of consumers where the relevant information is scattered over millions of individuals, who may not be aware of, or may not report, minor losses.

The lack of data explains the lack of guidance currently inherent in reasonableness standards.[42] To see how, suppose a court or legislature attempted to provide more guidance by specifying reasonably detailed standards for reasonable defense. It would be sheer accident if the standards came at all close to promoting a more or less close approximation of the consumer risk management

---

41 *Ibidem*, p. 484.
42 For an excellent discussion of current state of reasonableness standards, especially in regard to the Federal Trade Commission, Ch. J. Hoofnagle, *Federal Trade Commission Privacy Law and Policy*, 2016.

goal. To approximate that (other than by accident), one needs what is currently unavailable: reasonably reliable estimates of relevant magnitudes and probabilities. The promulgated standards would badly miss the mark by mandating too much or too little investment in defense. The only way to avoid this trap and impose a reasonableness standard is to do exactly what Smedinghoff notes the laws do: require reasonableness but provide little or no guidance about what would count as reasonable risk management.

The consequence is that the reasonableness standards fail to provide an adequate incentive to approximate the consumer risk management goal. The reason is that, in the network defense context, business can establish reasonableness by appeal to industry standards, and, as we noted earlier, those standards typically give insufficient weight to consumer losses. It is worth noting that allowing the appeal to industry standards is not necessarily a defect in the law. To see why, imagine you are a data holder. What practices should you adopt to defend consumers from harm from unauthorized access to your network? If you increase spending to improve security, you may lose business to competitors who do not do so. Consumers have been unwilling to pay for the added value of security through slightly higher retail prices or credit card fees. So, as a reasonable business person, what choice do you make? Like everyone else—everyone who remains in business—you choose to spend less. Your decision is the one a reasonable business person would make. Courts are reluctant to insist on an alternative decision when they lack the information necessary to explain why the alternative is better.

Some will rightly object that the law does not always bow in this way to industry standards. *The T. J. Hooper* is a classic example.[43] In March 1928, two tugboats, the *Montrose* and the *T. J. Hooper*, encountered a gale while towing barges up the Atlantic coast, and the tugs and the barges sank. The tugs did not have shortwave radios. Had they been so equipped, they would have received reports of the storm and put in at the Delaware breakwater to ride it out in safety. Shortwave radios, however, were new technology, and the industry standard was for tugs *not* to have one. The court nonetheless held that it was unreasonable not to equip the tug with a radio as a precaution against losses from storms. But note that risk management calculations are easy. It is obvious that the expected loss clearly exceeds the cost of the radio. Owners know that the losses, when they do occur, can be huge, and they know that, while the occurrence of violent storms is difficult to predict, their occurrence from time to time is certain. So

---

43 *T. J. Hooper*, 60 F. 2d 737, Circuit Court of Appeals, 2nd Circuit 1932.

tug boat owners should realize that adequate risk management means buying a radio. In contrast, the question about what adequate consumer risk management requires is unanswerable because the necessary information is currently unavailable. Rather than require answering the unanswerable, courts will defer to industry standards.

We think the best course is to turn the unanswerable question into an answerable one by taking steps to discover the necessary information. That may be a long and difficult road. Some may hope for an easier road to improving consumer risk management. Breach notification laws may appear to be just such a road.

3 Data breach notification laws

As the security expert Bruce Schneier notes, there are

> three reasons for breach notification laws. One, it's common politeness that when you lose something of someone else's, you tell him. The prevailing corporate attitude before the law – "They won't notice, and if they do notice they won't know it's us, so we are better off keeping quiet about the whole thing" – is just wrong. Two, it provides statistics to security researchers as to how pervasive the problem really is. And three, it forces companies to improve their security.[44]

We focus on the third reason. The laws certainly do lead businesses to increase security. The reason is that publicizing data breaches can impose significant costs on businesses,[45] and the threat of such losses has led businesses to increase online security.[46] Does the increase yield a more effective pursuit of the goal of consumer risk management?

We have found little relevant evidence, other than studies focusing on identity theft.[47] There is some evidence that the laws reduce identity theft. The identity theft studies correlate the existence of data breach laws with reductions in

---

44 B. Schneier, *State Data Breach Notification Laws: Have They Helped? Schneier on Security* (2009), https://www.schneier.com/essays/archives/2009/01/state_data_breach_no.html, last access: 26 April 2018.
45 Ponemon Cost of Data Breach Study: Global Analysis, 2916, p. 2.
46 *Ibidem*, p. 15.
47 David Thaw's work is an important exception. D. Thaw, *Data Breach (Regulatory) Effects*, 2015 Cardozo Law Rev. Novo 105, 163 (2015) (arguing that "an affirmative presumption of notification is superior from a cybersecurity perspective. Such a presumption avoids disincentivizing thorough cybersecurity investigations, which are one of the most important tools in protecting consumers against future data breaches and securing existing information systems").

identity theft. One cannot simply infer, however, that an increase in security is responsible for the reduction. Reductions in identity theft may result from of a variety of factors other than increased security.[48] In addition, even if the studies show that data-breach-law-motivated increases in security reduce identity theft that falls short of showing that they significantly improve consumer risk management. The reason is that the harm from unauthorized access reaches far beyond identity theft. It includes harm from ransomware, denial of services attacks, botnets engaged in fraud and other illegal activities, and viruses.[49] The available evidence is thus inconclusive at best.

There is, however, a general reason to doubt that data breach notification requirements improve consumer risk management. It emerges from considering the costs of compliance with notification requirements. Those costs include forensic and investigative activities, assessment and audit services, crisis team management, and communications to executive management and board of directors, notification costs, remediation activities, legal expenditures, product discounts, identity protection services and regulatory interventions, and lost business.[50] Data breach notification laws create an incentive to avoid *those* costs. It would be surprising if avoiding those *business* costs was strongly correlated with improved *consumer* risk management. Indeed, there is some reason to think such a correlation is unlikely. The reason is that the laws define the type of event a business must report.[51] They thus create an incentive to reduce *reportable* data breaches. They do not create an incentive to improve security in regard to problems that do not manifest themselves as reportable data breaches. As the law professor David Thaw notes, specific statutory regulations like data breach notifications laws can drive

> perhaps-otherwise-sufficient security budgets toward specific compliance objectives such as encryption. This, in turn, reduces the available resources for other security

---

48 R. Sullivan & J. Leigh Maniff, *Data Breach Notification Laws Kansas City Federal Reserve*, https://www.kansascityfed.org/~/media/files/publicat/econrev/econrevarchive/2016/1q16sullivanmaniff.pdf, last access: 26 April 2018.
49 Detica, *The Cost of Cybercrime 2* (Feb. 2011), http://www.cabinetoffice.gov.uk/sites/default/files/resources/the-cost-of-cyber-crime-full-report.pdf, last access: 26 April 2018.
50 *2016 Ponemon Cost of Data...*
51 Enterprise Information Security Group, Incident Handling and Breach Notification Center for Medicate & Medicad Services 1 (2012), https://www.cms.gov/research-statistics-data-and-systems/cms-information-technology/informationsecurity/downloads/rmh_viii_7-1_incident_handling_standard.pdf, last access: 26 April 2018.

activities, and forces CISOs to focus on meeting minimum compliance objectives rather than prioritizing the greatest threats they feel their organization faces. With an abundance of low-hanging fruit available to regulators – admittedly likely through malfeasance, not misfeasance – the bar is set extremely low. Thus regulators are faced with an "industry standard" set perhaps below their optimal level. As long as low-hanging fruit remains available to regulators, CISOs will not be able to justify requests for new resources on the grounds that peer organizations with comparable policies have been subject to enforcement action. Nor will they be able to justify requests based on the regulations themselves, as "reasonable" lacks an operational definition any higher than the low hanging fruit provided by cases [involving obvious and egregious security weaknesses] such as *B.J.'s Wholesale Club*, *T.J. Maxx Cos.*, and *Twitter*. And so the cycle continues.[52]

4 Conclusion

Data breach notification laws are an uncertain road to improving consumer risk management. The more certain, if longer, road to improving consumer risk management is to get the information risk management needs. This raises the question of how much data of what types of them are necessary for what purposes for how long. That question triggers possible privacy concerns.

---

52 D. Thaw, *Data Breach…*, p. 35.

LEX ET RES PUBLICA

POLISH LEGAL AND POLITICAL STUDIES

Edited by Anna Jarón

Vol. 1   Anna Jarón: Socio-Economic Constitutional Rights in Democratisation Processes. An Account of the Constitutional Dialogue Theory. 2012.

Vol. 2   Stanisław Filipowicz: Democracy – The Power of Illusion. 2013.

Vol. 3   Teresa Dukiet-Nagórska (ed.): The Postulates of Restorative Justice and the Continental Model of Criminal Law. As Illustrated by Polish Criminal Law 2014.

Vol. 4   Agnieszka Kupzok: Enforcement of Patents on Geographically Divisible Inventions. An Inquiry into the Standard of Substantive Patent Law Infringement in Cross-Border Constellations. 2015.

Vol. 5   Alicja Jagielska-Burduk / Wojciech Szafrański: Legal Issues in Cultural Heritage Management. A Polish Perspective. 2016.

Vol. 6   Maciej Mataczyński (ed.): The Takeover of Public Companies as a Mode of Exercising EU Treaty Free-doms. 2017.

Vol. 7   Maciej Barczewski (ed.): Value of Information: Intellectual Property, Privacy and Big Data. 2018.

www.peterlang.com

www.ingramcontent.com/pod-product-compliance
Ingram Content Group UK Ltd.
Pitfield, Milton Keynes, MK11 3LW, UK
UKHW021829210426
5322IPUK00004B/92